Caring for our world

A practical guide to ESD for ages 4-8

Fran Martin and Paula Owens

Geographical
Association

Acknowledgements

The authors would like to thank all the teachers and pupils from the schools mentioned in the book, as well as David Weatherley (Devon Curriculum Adviser for Geography and Education for Sustainable Development), Wendy North (Primary Projects Leader, Action Plan for Geography), Stephen Scoffham (Principal Lecturer at Canterbury Christ University) and Geraint Bevan (Humanities Adviser for Carmarthenshire).

Many thanks also to all those who supplied the photos used throughout the book.

Cover image and chapter illustrations are taken from the work of pupils at Ammanford Infants.

Photos

Photographs from contributing schools have been used interchangeably to illustrate chapters where appropriate.

Page 4-5: Jane Whittle; 7-10: Paula Owens; 12: Cohdra/Morguefile; 13: missyredboots/Morguefile; 14: Paula Owens, Georgina Pope; 15: Georgina Pope; 16: Sideshowmom/Morguefile, Robb Kiser/Morguefile; 18: missyredboots/Morguefile; 19: Jane Whittle, Fran Martin; 20: kakisky/Morguefile; 21: clarita/Morguefile; 22: demondimum/Morguefile, Jane Whittle; 23: Jane Whittle; 24: digiology/Morguefile; 25: Jane Whittle, monosodium/Morguefile; 26: Paula Owens; 27: Fran Martin, Paula Owens; 28: dieraecherin/Morguefile; 29: Forest School Shropshire – Shropshire County Council; 30: Fran Martin, Forest School Shropshire – Shropshire County Council; 31-2: Fran Martin; 33: Fran Martin, Paula Owens; 34: Jane Whittle, biberta/Morguefile; 35: mantasmagorical/Morguefile, Forest School Shropshire – Shropshire County Council; 36-45: Paula Owens; 46: I melenchon/Morguefile; 47: The Ashden Awards for Sustainable Energy; 48: Briar Arnold/Eastchurch School; 49: The Ashden Awards for Sustainable Energy; 51: Briar Arnold/Eastchurch School; 52: The Ashden Awards for Sustainable Energy, Jim McManners; 53: The Ashden Awards for Sustainable Energy; 54-55: Diane Wright;56: Paula Owens, Diane Wright; 57: Paula Owens; 58: Fran Martin, Paula Owens, 59: Jane Whittle, Paula Owens; 60: ladyheart/Morguefile; 61-62: Fran Martin.

ISBN 978-1-84377-211-8
First published 2008
Impression number 10 9 8 7 6 5 4 3 2 1
Year 2010 2009 2008

Published by the Geographical Association, 160 Solly Street, Sheffield S1 4BF
Website: www.geography.org.uk
E-mail: info@geography.org.uk
The Geographical Association is a registered charity: no 313129.
The Publications Officer of the GA would be happy to hear from other potential authors who have ideas for geography books. You may contact the Officer via the GA at the address above. The views expressed in this publication are those of the authors and do not necessarily represent those of the Geographical Association.
Editing: Dorcas Turner
Design and typesetting: Ledgard Jepson
Printing and binding: In China through Colorcraft Ltd, Hong Kong

Contents

Foreword

Caring for Our World is a very timely and important resource and I would recommend it to all primary teachers, not just those of geography. Why? Because it expands our ideas about what we are teaching for and how we must go about it. This is especially important at the age level covered in this book, as the current 4-8-year-olds will live through changes we cannot predict and may even end up in careers that do not yet exist. All we can say for sure is that the world will be different and change will occur. This doesn't diminish us as teachers, however. Rather, it provides the springboard into real and authentic dialogue with our pupils, where lifelong competencies and skills are learnt. As a teacher and outdoor educator, my real moments of joy were when I felt I was learning as much as the pupils.

Teaching and engaging with today's pupils about unknown and possible futures is essential and requires different teaching techniques. These may include socially-critical thinking (how did we get here?), action learning (to build confidence in 'having a go' at sustainable development), or creative and joined-up thinking (sometimes called 'systems thinking' or 'linking thinking'). While these techniques are good teaching practice in any subject, they are vital for sustainable development thinking: action learning and reflecting on what has been learnt are crucial to building capable citizens and confident learners. It goes beyond hands-on learning, or even some interpretations of experiential learning. The key words here are reflection and learning to learn. This book is full of examples of this.

The content for sustainable development will keep changing. When I studied climate change at postgraduate level, the only climate change that was talked about was the next ice-age – and I am not that old! However, the ESD topics that won't change will be about our impact on our planet, our communities and each other, both locally and globally. We may use transport as a theme, but the story about why we have certain transport modes and how we make choices is crucial to understanding about how to make different choices in the future.

It is a breath of fresh air to read the voices and case studies that show that this is not a book about telling pupils to turn off lights! In fact, pupils are very clear about how they like to learn – in groups, doing practical things, with friends and by using computers, and this is exactly how ESD should be learnt.

Finally, ESD, and in particular the DCSF's Sustainable Schools initiative, is for the whole school as this is the only way to sustain it. While you are learning with and from the students, you may also want to be learning and reflecting with your colleagues. Surely the experience pupils will get from the topics and ideas contained in this book shouldn't be limited to the class of one enthusiastic teacher for one year? Instead, it should be progressed year-on-year so that pupils can constantly develop their understanding and competencies. Actually, I will go further: I think it is every pupil's right.

Ann Finlayson
Commissioner – Education and Capability Building
Sustainable Development Commission

Introduction

We are currently surrounded by reports that our world is in crisis. Climate change, social injustice, war, and unfair distribution and over-consumption of precious resources are all changing the world as we know it. It is imperative that we ensure that today's pupils have the knowledge and skills to prevent the escalation of problems and the ability to respond to the changes as they happen. We already know that changes have to be made to the way we lead our lives but it is daunting to think about the problems let alone identify workable solutions. However, we do not have the luxury of standing and doing nothing. So what can we do?

As Nelson Mandela said: 'Education is the most powerful weapon you can use to change the world'. As teachers, we must play a key part in educating pupils for the possible futures they may face and give them the skills to tackle the problems of today and tomorrow. This is perhaps the most important challenge we face – to ensure that today's generation of young people are well-informed, have the necessary skills and are motivated to understand why and how they can live their lives in more sustainable ways.

When writing a practical guide about how to teach education for sustainable development (ESD) in the Early Years, some discussion about what this actually means may be needed first. There is much debate about ESD, and through our experiences as deputy head teachers, curriculum advisors and teacher educators, we have realised that similar questions keep cropping up. For this reason we have decided to take a 'Frequently Asked Questions' approach in this introduction.

what is education for sustainable development (ESD)?

Before you can answer this question it is necessary to consider:

What is sustainable development?

There are over 300 definitions of sustainable development but one that you may be familiar with is:

> "Development that meets the needs of the present without compromising the ability of future generations to meet their own needs (Brundtland, 1987)."

The original online National Curriculum 2000 support materials, however, used these definitions:

> "Sustainable means that something is viable and can be continued in the long term in ways that do not harm people but benefit them equally. This can apply to anything from decisions about the school playground to issues relating to the national economy and global environment"

and

> "Development refers to the way in which the interaction between the environment, the economy and society progresses and changes. Development happens everywhere and involves everyone."

More recently, when commenting on the Sustainable Schools programme, Bill Scott (2006), head of the Centre for Research in Environmental Education at the University of Bath, said:

> "It embodies the key idea that the way humans are living threatens the planet's ability to support us."

Why so many definitions?

When you look at these (and other) definitions, there are a lot of common elements: they all have a futures dimension and they all hint at the fact that the way in which we currently live cannot be supported by the planet's resources in the long term.

However, while all the definitions agree that it is necessary to think about the future, your vision for the future may differ greatly to that of the person next to you. We all have conflicting needs and wants but have come to realise that because we live in a connected world we need to consider the effect of our actions, not just on ourselves but on others and the global environment which we share. Sustainable development is a process: thinking about ourselves, thinking about others and using our knowledge to make responsible decisions and actions. Crucially, it is about recognising that when thinking about the future our knowledge is at best uncertain so any decisions need to incorporate a critical and cautious approach.

What do we need to think about?

If sustainable development were a three-legged stool (as in Figure 1), the legs would represent economy, environment and society. When thinking about the sustainability of any development all three need to be taken into account because without any one support the stool would collapse. The examples in this book show how although all three elements are always present, there are times when one must be emphasised more than the others.

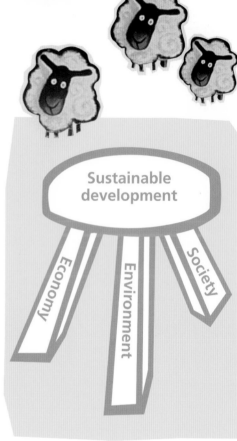

Figure 1: The three elements of sustainability.

Where does the 'education' come into it?

ESD is about developing pupils' knowledge, values and skills to enable the above to be achieved. Like sustainable development itself, it is a process of participation. It is not about telling pupils what to do or believe; it is about developing their capacity to make responsible decisions for themselves (an example is given in Table 1).

The Sustainable Schools strategy says that ESD is about developing respect and care for oneself, others and the environment at three different scales: curriculum, campus and community.

ESD	Not ESD
Lessons that compare fair trade with organic and non fair trade products and balance different needs (environment, economy, society) to allow pupils to come to personal decisions about whether to buy fair trade or not.	Lessons on fair trade that 'lead' pupils to the conclusion that buying fair trade products is the right thing to do.

Table 1: What is ESD?

The ladder of participation for sustainable development

Learning through an ongoing spiral of:
Awareness
(through gaining knowledge)
Understanding
(comprehension and forming own opinions)
Application and evaluation
(taking action and evaluating that action)

Issues, such as those in the following chapters, provide a real and meaningful context for this work which in turn can make a real contribution to the life of the class, school, and community.

Take action

Form opinions

Develop skills and understanding

Gain knowledge

Figure 2: Spiral of progression.

Why should I teach ESD?

On current projections humanity will be using two planets worth of natural resources by 2050 – if those resources have not run out by then – as 'people are turning resources into waste faster than nature can turn waste back into resources' (WWF, 2006).

To enable teachers to implement ESD more confidently there have been a range of government-led initiatives. In Wales ESD and Global Citzenship (ESDGC) is a combined initiative whereas in Scotland ESD is embedded in the curriculum and their plans for the UN Decade of ESD have been published as *Learning for Our Future* (2006). In England ESD is being promoted through the Sustainable Schools strategy. This is good news for schools, as Bill Scott (2006) observes:

> It seems to me that the DfES is encouraging schools to have an outward looking and future focussed curriculum that enables children to engage in open-ended ways with the hugely significant debates that are happening in the wider world, the outcomes of which will surely affect their lives. This is an educational vision presented by the challenge of sustainable development.

Are there any other reasons?

Yes. ESD has been a statutory part of the geography, science and design and technology National Curriculum orders since 2000. Furthermore, ESD is explicitly mentioned in the over-arching aims and purposes of the National Curriculum as a whole:

> [The school curriculum] should develop [pupils'] awareness and understanding of, and respect for, the environments in which they live, and secure their commitment to sustainable development at a personal, local, national and global level (DfEE/QCA 1999).

Is there a danger that pupils will feel overburdened by these problems?

Holden (2007) has shown that pupils as young as seven are already concerned about things they hear about in the news, such as war and climate change, as well as things they have personal experience of, such as bullying and local issues. To ignore these concerns is to ignore part of the knowledge and understanding pupils bring with them to school and this could lead to the formation of attitudes that will be much harder to address later on. Also, as will be outlined below, ESD is not only about raising awareness of issues; it is also about pupils considering alternative solutions and choosing paths of action that start with themselves at a local level. This gives them a sense of empowerment and the realisation that they can make a difference. All the examples in this book will illustrate this.

ESD concept	Learning implications for 4–8-year-olds
1. Citizenship and stewardship Gaining the skills, knowledge and understanding to become informed, global citizens, recognising that we all have rights and responsibilities to participate in decision making and that everyone should have a say in what happens in the future	Develop through a spiral of ongoing awareness, understanding, application and evaluation: • the skills needed to exercise the power of choice that exists in many aspects of everyday decision making • care for oneself and others at increasingly complex scales, i.e. home, school and local environments • the knowledge and skills needed for involvement in simple democratic processes: e.g. planning actions with other members of the school community, electing classroom and school monitors and councillors • a growing sense of responsibility and capacity for action, e.g. working with others to make suggestions and take action
2. Interdependence Understanding that people, places and environments are all interrelated at local and global level, and that decisions taken in one place have repercussions elsewhere	Develop through a spiral of ongoing awareness, understanding, application and evaluation: • the knowledge that all living things depend on each other, and that what people do affect themselves, the places they live, other people, plants and animals • an appreciation of how simple everyday events link to the wider world and how we are a part of this process • the knowledge that individual and collective actions and events have impacts at different scales
3. Needs and rights of future generations Knowing about human rights and learning how to lead lives that consider the rights and needs of others, and that what we do now has implications for what life will be like in the future	Develop through a spiral of ongoing awareness, understanding, application and evaluation: • the ability to recognise our own basic needs, i.e. shelter, warmth and food, and begin to think about essential and non-essential needs • careful thinking about why we all have similar needs which are often met in unequal ways • an appreciation that our basic needs are met by goods and services provided by people using natural resources • the ability to distinguish between products that are wasteful and those that are more sustainable • the knowledge that some natural resources are finite while others can be used sustainably
4. Diversity Understanding the importance and value of diversity in our lives – culturally, socially, economically and biologically	Develop through a spiral of ongoing awareness, understanding, application and evaluation: • the knowledge that different natural environments have different groups of animals and plants • the ability to respect and value other peoples and cultures and their diverse views and opinions • a disposition towards open-mindedness • a growing sense of what is meant by biodiversity in local and global contexts and the importance of maintaining biodiversity at these levels
5. Quality of life Recognising that for development to be sustainable it must benefit people in an equitable way and improve the welfare of all people	Develop through a spiral of ongoing awareness, understanding, application and evaluation: • an understanding of what quality of life means and what components it might have • an appreciation of the basic difference between needs and wants • the ability to recognise and question unfairness and inequality in the way that resources are distributed • thinking about ways in which resources can be shared out more fairly
6. Sustainable change Understanding that there is a limit to the way the world can develop and that consequences of unsustainable growth are increased poverty and degradation of the environment	Develop through a spiral of ongoing awareness, understanding, application and evaluation: • a sense of responsibility about the ways in which our actions affect the environment • the knowledge that some of our actions may harm the world around us • a growing sense of how our actions might safeguard aspects of the world around us that we choose to protect • the knowledge that some resources may run out (finite) whilst others can be replenished or renewed • the ability to question the effect of our actions at different scales on the wider world, both now and in the future
7. Uncertainty and precaution Recognising that we are learning all the time and we should adopt a cautious approach to the welfare of the planet as our actions may have unforeseen consequences	Develop through a spiral of ongoing awareness, understanding, application and evaluation: • an appreciation of how important is it to consider the consequences of our actions • individual and collaborative ideas as to how localities at different scales may be managed more sustainably • the sense that there are a range of possible futures and uncertain outcomes that we have the power to affect • growing confidence in our ability to engage with a range of everyday problems

Adapted from: Holland Report, 1998.

Table 2: The seven concepts of ESD and learning implications.

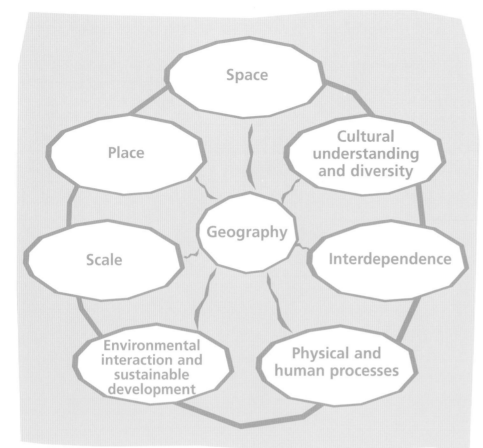

Figure 3: The Key Concepts of geography.

If ESD is a concept that underpins the whole curriculum, why is the GA publishing this book?

The Key Concepts of geography (Figure 3) have many elements common to those underpinning ESD. This is not to say that if you are doing geography you are automatically doing ESD, but if you are doing ESD then you are probably doing geography! Geography is a good lens through which to focus an interdisciplinary approach to ESD because it involves learning about the world in everyday contexts and at different scales, demands participative and enquiry-led skills, and takes an interconnected view of local and global events. These kinds of skills and attributes are vital aspects of ESD.

As already mentioned, ESD is written into the National Curriculum geography orders. At KS1 this focuses on developing pupils' understanding of environmental change and recognition of how the environment can be improved and sustained.

I don't have time to teach yet another initiative

In recent years there have been a number of strategies, initiatives and policies affecting primary schools: Excellence and Enjoyment: A primary national strategy, Every Child Matters (ECM), Social and Emotional Aspects of Learning (SEAL), Personalised Learning and the report on creativity and its contribution to these agendas. ESD could be perceived as just another initiative in this long list. However, apart from the fact that ESD is written into the National Curriculum, it is also an umbrella concept with an approach to teaching and learning that has the potential to tie all these initiatives together. A better understanding of ESD will support teachers in meeting the targets of the other agendas, as is explained below.

ESD and Every Child Matters
ESD is an integral part of ECM. As Simon Catling (2007) observes: 'the government sees the five ECM outcomes as almost providing a "blueprint for child-centred sustainable development"'. Examples of how ESD can contribute to the five ECM outcomes are outlined in Table 3.

How do I teach ESD?

This book provides practical, everyday examples of how to teach ESD in ways that are appropriate for pupils in the Early Years but an essential starting point is to familiarise yourself with the key concepts of ESD. This is important because they underpin all of our thinking in ESD.

Table 2 has brief descriptions of the concepts identified by the Holland Report (1998), and some of the learning implications that we envisage arising from this. In our examples we show how teaching these concepts in synergy will work better than attempting to teach them separately.

Each of the learning implications in Table 2 refers to a 'spiral of ongoing awareness, understanding, application and evaluation' because we believe that even pupils as young as five are capable of applying what they have learnt in everyday contexts, albeit at simplistic levels (Martin and Owens, 2004). Progression is achieved as pupils revisit this cycle of awareness, moving into action with ever increasing levels of complexity (see Figure 2).

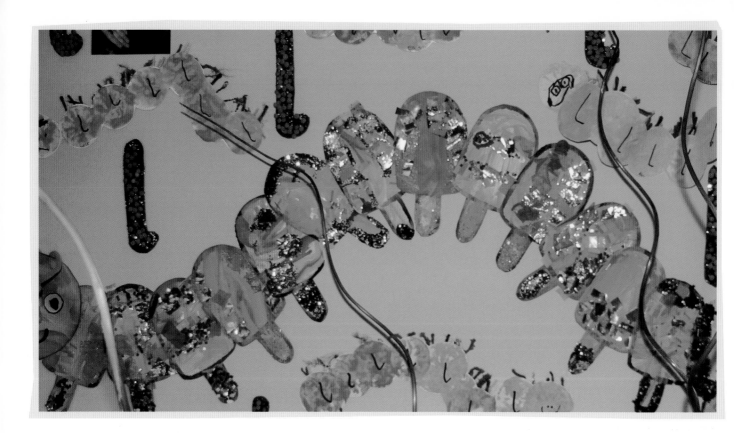

ECM outcomes	How ESD can contribute
Be healthy	ESD teaches pupils to recognise the distinction between needs and wants as part of their understanding of what constitutes a healthy lifestyle. Understanding physical, mental and emotional health is an integral part of understanding the key concept of quality of life
Stay safe	Through ESD pupils learn about health and safety issues, risk assessments and the use of common sense when working in outdoor environments. Pupils debate what counts as anti-social behaviour in the context of their interactions with the environment
Enjoy and achieve	Pupils gain a great sense of achievement when they are involved in decision-making processes which relate to their real-world experiences and concerns. When these are used as curriculum examples pupils' motivation levels, and therefore achievement, are potentially much greater
Make a positive contribution to society	ESD is action orientated. Action in school can have a positive impact on the local community, and the local community can make a positive contribution through active involvement in school projects
Achieve economic well-being	ESD encourages pupils to consider the distribution of resources, both locally and globally. Through topics such as energy, travel and food they develop an understanding of how to use resources wisely. The skills, knowledge and understanding developed through ESD are those required to be active and responsible global citizens

Table 3: ESD and ECM.

ESD and Personalised Learning

The then DfES (2007) defined personalised learning as that which enables 'all children and young people, whatever their starting point, ... to fulfil their potential as learners' (p. 8). They suggested that this is something that also requires organisational structures at school (campus) and wider community level to support it.

A guiding principle of sustainable development, and therefore ESD, is to enable development of life on the planet that is equitable for all, to enable all to achieve a better quality of life, and to do so without compromising the ability of future generations to do the same. Recognising the importance of each individual component as well as the interdependent nature of all the components is therefore central to both personalised learning and ESD.

ESD and SEAL

Recent research into how the brain functions has been having an increasing impact on education. We are now much more aware of how learning that appeals to the emotions as well as the intellect is more likely to be longer lasting than that which is purely cognitive. The SEAL programme aims to develop the qualities and skills that promote positive behaviour and effective learning. It focuses on five social and emotional aspects of learning: self-awareness, managing feelings, motivation, empathy and social skills. Successful ESD involves all these elements. Care, as highlighted above, is a core value of ESD (care for self, others and environment).

ESD and creativity

We live in an uncertain and changing world. How we expect the world to change affects the way we live our lives today. When we consider what is probable we should also envision what is possible and what we would prefer. Thinking about the future in this way is a creative act which involves using imagination, speculating about possibilities, considering alternatives and comparing ideas. It also raises questions about values. There is a real sense that we can create the future that we want if only we have the vision to imagine it (Scoffham and Dorman, 2007).

As Fisher (2004) notes, 'Imagination can be used to serve evil ends so it needs to be informed by values [in this case, the values that underpin ESD and the key concepts]. Imagination can lead to false belief so it needs to be tempered by critical thinking, reasoning and judgement'. Table 4 provides a useful overview of the difference between creative and critical thinking.

Creative thinking	Critical thinking
synthesis	analysis
divergent	convergent
possibility	probability
imagination	judgment
hypothesis forming	hypothesis testing
subjective	objective
open-ended	closed
speculating	reasoning
intuitive	logical
yes and	yes but

Table 4: Creative and critical thinking.

What is in this book?

Each chapter in this book has real examples drawn from a range of primary schools. Across the six chapters we have used the same framework and aimed to cover the ESD concepts, the eight 'doorways' of the Sustainable Schools strategy, the five ECM outcomes and various aspects of other initiatives. We have also identified how each example links to other areas of the curriculum.

References

Bruntland, G. (1987) *Our Common Future: The World Commission on Environment and Development.* Oxford: Oxford University Press.

Catling, S. (2007) 'ECM6 = environmental well-being?', *Primary Geographer*, 63, pp. 5-8.

Cremin, T., Barnes, J. and Scoffham, S. (2007) *Creative Teaching for Tomorrow: Fostering a creative state of mind.* A research study undertaken for Creative Partnerships (Kent) by Canterbury Christ Church University, unpublished.

DfEE/QCA (1999) *The National Curriculum for England.* London: HMSO.

DfES (2007) *PNS: Pedagogy and personalisation.* London: DfES.

Fisher, R. (2004) 'What is creativity?', in Fisher, R. and Williams, M. (eds) *Unlocking Creativity: A teacher's guide to creativity across the curriculum.* London: David Fulton.

Holden, C. (2007) 'Young people's concerns', in Hicks, D. and Holden, C. (eds) *Teaching the Global Dimension: Key principles and effective practice.* Abingdon: Routledge.

Holland, G. (1998) *A Report to DfEE/QCA on Education for Sustainable Development in the Schools Sector from the Panel for Education for Sustainable Development.* Available at *www.defra.gov.uk/environment/sustainable/educpanel/1998ar/ann4.htm*

Martin, F. and Owens, P. (2004) 'Children making sense of their place in the world', in Scoffham, S. (ed) *Primary Geography Handbook.* Sheffield: Geographical Association, pp. 62-73.

Scoffham, S. and Dorman, P. (2007) 'Multiple perspectives, profound understandings', *Primary Geographer*, 64, pp. 31-3.

Scottish Executive (2006) *Learning for Our Future: Scotland's first action plan for the UN decade of education for sustainable development.* Edinburgh: Scottish Executive.

Scott, B. (2006) *ESD. What sort of decade? What sort of learning?* Keynote address at the UK launch of the UNESCO Decade for ESD, unpublished.

WWF (2006) *Living Planet Report 2006.* Available online at *www.panda.org/news_facts/publications/living_planet_report/index.cfm*

Useful websites

www.esd-wales.org.uk/
Education for Sustainable Development and Global Citizenship in Wales.

www.everychildmatters.gov.uk/
Every Child Matters online.

www.geographyteachingtoday.org.uk/
Geography Teaching Today. Follow links for 'KS1–3 courses' and 'Primary geography and ESD' for online CPD and supporting resources.

www.ltscotland.org.uk/sustainabledevelopment/index.asp
Learning and Teaching Scotland. Sustainable development education advice and resources.

www.standards.dfes.gov.uk/personalisedlearning/
Personalised learning online.

www.standards.dfes.gov.uk/primary/publications/banda/seal/
The SEAL programme online.

www.teachernet.gov.uk/sustainableschools/
The Sustainable Schools strategy (England).

www.wmnet.org.uk/wmnet/22.cfm
Follow the 'teachers', 'curriculum links', 'curriculum overview' links for a downloadable file showing how ESD (in this example climate change) can contribute to learning across the curriculum, and how curriculum subjects can contribute to learning about climate change.

Growing Schools

How does our garden grow?

This chapter (along with those on Forest School (pp. 28-35) and Food and Farming (pp. 20-27)) shows how using the outdoors in lessons can help pupils to connect to the world that they live in and that sustains them. It also has a strong community element to it.

Key ESD concepts

- interdependence
- diversity
- quality of life

Subject links

- science
- geography
- citizenship

Other links

ECM 1: Be healthy
ECM 4: Make a positive contribution
SEAL: Pupils gain emotionally, intellectually and physically; they develop emotional attachment to their garden which increases their levels of environmental concern.

Planned outcomes

- Interdependence: an appreciation that the garden could not be maintained without the involvement of the whole community; an understanding of the role of the garden in the school's community.
- Citizenship and stewardship: skills in planning and looking after the garden, in negotiating and sharing roles, and in making decisions about the garden and how the produce could be shared; a sense of care and responsibility through fulfilling commitments made to digging and weeding as well as reaping the rewards at harvest time.
- Diversity: an understanding, through trial and error, of what to grow, how to grow it and therefore a greater understanding of biodiversity locally and globally.
- Quality of life: an understanding of the time, effort and money it takes to keep a small garden productive and therefore a greater appreciation of the processes involved in producing the food that might otherwise be taken for granted; a sense of pride in and appreciation/enjoyment of the produce from the garden.

Other geography outcomes

- use of mapping skills in garden designs
- understanding of microclimates and their effect on plants' growth.
- understanding of weather and climate: seasonal variations in crops, what can be grown in the UK and what can't.

Unplanned outcomes

- Opportunities to solve real-life problems: gardening is not an exact science and pupils need to learn how to apply problem-solving skills to cope with unexpected problems as they arise.

Essential resources

- An area that can be developed and sustained as a school garden
- Teachers, pupils, parents and others in the local community who are willing to commit to making the garden viable in the long term
- Gardening equipment (e.g. unwanted tools donated by parents)
- Seeds
- Funds (see how Chaddesley Corbett Primary School funded their garden below)
- Enthusiasm!

Starting points

Chaddesley Corbett Primary School is located in a rural area, where roughly half the pupils come from the immediate locality, with some being the offspring of farmers and market gardeners, while the other half come from the urban areas of Kidderminster. As a consequence, some pupils are real experts on their environment and have a developed understanding of what needs to be done to protect it, while others have little or no connection with their environment and see the world around them as something 'out there' rather than something they actually live in.

> " Our starting point was the run-down and neglected wildlife area which was no longer used by the school. The area is huge and we had to think about what was realistically manageable. After initial discussions we decided to keep a large part of the area for wildlife, another for Forest School activities (see chapter 3 for an example of this) and to use the remaining area, which was about the size of an average allotment, for a school garden. "

Prompt questions

- What do you want to grow?
- How do you grow this?
- Is it possible to grow this in Britain?
- How would you protect it from the cold weather?

When their plants didn't grow as expected …

- Why do you think this has happened?
- What could be changed?
- How could you make it easier for your plant to grow?
- What could we do differently next year?

These questions were raised in response to the different problems as and when they arose. They encourage pupils, where possible, to find the solutions for themselves.

Activities and challenges

A key principle in sustaining a school garden is ownership by the whole community. Giving pupils ownership of the garden design created enormous enthusiasm for joining the gardening club and, once it was established, for using the garden for curriculum activities.

Garden designs

> All pupils in the school were invited to take part in the garden design competition. They were given some formal input into what an organic garden is, and told that in their school they were going to use traditional gardening methods and why this was the case. To help their thinking they compared gardening methods in the UK with those in The Gambia, the location of their link school. Photographs of a Gambian school's banana and vegetable garden were shown, with examples of methods used for watering, keeping beetles off the carrots, and the composting area which provides nutrients for the garden. Pupils were then given a set of criteria for their design: it had to have a composting area, a plot large enough to use a vegetable garden, a means of water collection so it would not use the school's water resources, and a wildlife area. The designs were judged by a teacher, a parent and the school's eco-committee which has a pupil representative from each class.

Getting stuck in

Once the garden was up and running an after-school gardening club was established. It now meets once a week and pupils get down to the business of tending and maintaining the garden. In the beginning the club was very much teacher led as Sally Wood describes:

> Initially I had a large amount of input into what, where and how we should grow things. As the pupils' skills developed, however, I took much more of a back seat and let them discover things for themselves. Small groups were formed and each was responsible for a patch where they could grow whatever they wanted. We had some wonderfully ambitious projects, such as pineapples, mangoes and other tropical plants. The pupils then went away and researched why the plants weren't growing well in their garden. It was a joy to listen to them discussing how to protect their plants from the cold, slugs and rabbits and there were some very interesting ideas for traps and deterrents! There were also many interesting conversations between the children of farmers and the 'townies' as to why we couldn't grow a pineapple successfully over winter. We've had some very successful experiments as well, such as growing kilos and kilos of potatoes in buckets because we didn't want to take up valuable growing space.

I can't wait to eat them!

we've found a great way to support our peas!

Buying and selling

At their own request, pupils have learned how the market place works. They sold off their glut of tomato plants early in the year, undercutting competition from the local nursery by about 50%! They have also sold fruit and vegetables after school, given produce to the harvest festival, and donated some of the money raised to causes such as a local women's refuge centre. Other profits have been ploughed back into the garden to buy seeds, composting bins, guttering for collecting rainwater and other equipment to make their garden more successful and sustainable.

Challenges for pupils

A variety of different challenges have been provided both for and by pupils. At the design stage the challenge was to find the most creative yet practical way of working within the strict criteria. This used the range of creative and critical thinking skills referred to in the introduction of this book. In the growing stage, pupils often challenged themselves through their choices of what to grow and how to grow it, and also through the trial and error process. They were wonderfully inventive about solutions to a range of unexpected problems that arose, as the example below indicates. The fact that this is their garden and they have ownership of it, with only sensitive guidance from their teacher, has meant that every week has brought its own challenges.

How pupils responded to the following challenge is a good indication of how this ownership has led to a huge sense of pride and attachment to their garden.

Garden under threat

A recent suggestion by governors to place a much needed mobile classroom on the garden was quickly and eloquently argued against by the pupils. They first went to the headteacher to inform her of their views, then ensured that the parent governors were made aware of the situation, before finally writing a letter expressing their concerns to the governing body. They were overjoyed when the suggestion was withdrawn and they had learnt a valuable lesson about the democratic process.

Challenges for teachers

Sally described how:

At first there was a lot of interest and help but this quickly dropped off when helpers realised they were required in all weathers and temperatures! I was quickly left with just the hardened enthusiasts, which was often only me, the pupils and one granddad. Funding for the garden was also a huge challenge but I quickly learned who to approach: our local environmental studies centre provides courses on raising funds for school grounds; independent organisations such as Alan Titchmarsh Gardens for Schools provide grants; and companies such as B&Q often let schools have end-of-line tools etc. for free when they want to clear their shelves. There's also Freecycle where you can swap and 'beg' items, and if you enrol with the Henry Doubleday Research Association (see *www.gardenorganic.org.uk/organicgardening/schools.php*) they will send you free seeds and a link to their website which gives advice and activities for rainy days. Of course the paperwork involved in all of this can take up a lot of time so you may need to enlist another adult who does not want to be involved in the practical side of the garden, but does want to help in some way.

The summer holiday normally hails the start of the harvesting season so you (or a willing volunteer) will need to be constantly picking lettuces, tomatoes, summer cabbages, spinach, etc. during your precious holiday time. Other issues to think about include who will water and weed the garden over the summer and Easter holidays so it's not a jungle when you return. These can be major problems to solve if there are no willing parents or staff around to assist.

Having said that, it really is worth it in the end!

Vocabulary

Garden, soil, compost, organic, names of different vegetables (e.g. lettuces, cabbages, carrots, potatoes, tomatoes), seasons, names of different animals affecting the garden (e.g. slugs, rabbits, worms), names of gardening tools (e.g. spade, fork, trowel, hoe).

Pupils' voices

This is one example of the pupils' conversations that shows just how much they were thinking and challenging each other:

Oh no! All our lettuces have gone!

That's rabbits.

Let's get a rabbit trap.

No! we don't want to hurt them!

How can we get rid of them then?

Let's block the lettuces off with a fence.

No! The rabbits can dig underneath.

I know, we can cover the plants to stop the rabbits getting to them.

Let's try using plant pots.

The pupils agreed to try using up-turned plant pots to cover the lettuces, but as they carefully placed them over what was left of their lettuces they noticed:

Look, there's no light getting in. They need light to grow.

what else can we use?

It needs to be see through.

my dad's got some of those plastic things [cloches]. I'll ask if we can have them.

"

The pupils have thrown themselves wholeheartedly into the project and they now share all their information and ideas. I have tried to ensure that all groups have pupils with experience so that they can work as independently as possible. We try to discuss our failings and successes and share tips with each other. The project very successfully crosses all ability levels. It is wonderful to watch pupils' faces when they see a potato come out of the ground for the first time, or when they discover peas in a pod and taste them raw. Pupils with learning difficulties in the classroom have quickly grown in confidence as many realise that they really 'know their stuff' out in the garden. Listening as pupils problem solve without thinking about it and exchange ideas and advice with peers who they would not normally listen to them, with their confidence growing along with the garden, is pure joy! A huge sense of pride in the garden has been developed and pupils appear to have learned to truly love their patch. Any stray piece of litter that dares to enter the garden is met with complete outrage – how dare anyone spoil their land?!

"

Futures perspectives

Futures thinking is integral to the processes involved in the garden. The pupils have become very good at forward planning and trying to anticipate seasonal variations and how to adapt to them. They are also learning to deal with uncertainty and precaution taking on a regular basis, even though they now know that no matter how hard they think about what might happen and carefully plan for it, there is always something unexpected that turns up that means they have to think again.

Further ideas

The garden is no longer used only by the after school group but is in much demand as a resource to enrich the curriculum. Maths lessons now takes place there with pupils measuring the length of beds, calculating how many carrots are in a row and working out the multiplication that has taken place from one potato. Literacy also uses the garden, exploring the senses, listening to the sounds, describing the scent of a freshly dug carrot or crushed herb, and science lessons are brought to life: growing, exploring, enquiring. The list of how the garden can be used is endless.

Teacher reflections

The conversation above is just one of many examples of how different previous experiences enabled pupils to solve their own problems and challenge each others' ideas. Here, the farmers' children understood from personal experience that rabbits will dig under anything that is put in their path in order to get to vegetables! These pupils were also less worried about the rabbits and more concerned for the produce, whereas those from a non-farming background were determined that the rabbits should not be harmed.

" In year 1 the garden is mainly used as an outdoor space for art and science lessons, although it has also been used for maths and measuring as well. The private nursery on the site has recently asked me if they can have a little patch of the garden for their children to grow plants in and explore, and the key stage 2 pupils from the school have asked if I could start a gardening club for them in their 'golden choice' time (when they can choose to do whatever activities they wish for an hour). "

Assessment for Learning

Due to the trial and error nature of the venture, this is a wonderful example of how pupils are self and peer assessing the whole time and, because things will not grow if they don't persevere and learn from their mistakes, the motivation to keep going and get it right is enormous!

Why we chose this

This is a project that can be easily replicated, either on a whole-school or individual class scale. You don't necessarily have to have a large plot – window boxes can be used to grow a variety of food! This example illustrates opportunities for inclusive learning and shows how pupils' confidence grows as they transform planning into direct action.

References and further resources

Websites

www.teachernet.gov.uk/growingschools/
Teachernet's growing schools website gives advice about 'making it happen', as well as teaching resources and activity ideas.

www.schoolsgarden.org.uk/resources/ resources.asp
This teachers' pack from a schools garden venture at Hampton Court Flower Show provides a range of ideas that link to many areas of the curriculum.

www.alantitchmarsh.com/gardensfor schools.asp
Awards of up to £500 are made each year.

Fiction books

Carle, E. (1997) *The Tiny Seed*. London: Puffin Books.

French, V. and Bartlett, A. (1995) *Oliver's Vegetables*. London: Hodder Children's Books.

French, V. and Bartlett, A. (1998) *Oliver's Fruit Salad*. London: Hodder Children's Books.

Krauss, R. (1945) *The Carrot Seed*. London: HarperCollins.

Parkinson, K. (1986) *The Enormous Turnip*. Morton Grove, IL: Albert Whitman and Company.

Potter, B. (2002) *The Tale of Peter Rabbit* (New edition). Frederick Warne and Co.

making Scarecrows

Jane Whittle describes some practical measures taken by pupils at Edwalton Primary School in Nottingham to safeguard their vegetable plot.

Resources

- old clothes
- straw
- string
- stakes for fixing into ground.

A handsome bunch!

Guarding the allotment!

"The pupils needed to take precautionary measures because of a threat to their vegetables from marauding birds. Working together, they were able to take responsible action and enact some practical stewardship by making scarecrows to safeguard their hard work.

They were given a pile of old clothes and asked to assemble an outfit for their group's scarecrow. The sleeves of the shirts and legs of the trousers were then tied up with string and the clothes were stuffed with straw.

The stitching and securing to the stakes was done by adults and the scarecrows put into the school allotment."

Getting Started

Thomas and Sharelle Vandborg are joint co-ordinators for ESD at Ilfracombe Infant and Nursery School in North Devon. They are leading a project to develop the outdoor classroom as part of an overall programme to improve ESD at the school, and share their ideas here.

Mission statement: We aim to produce understanding citizens of the twenty-first century who recognise the need to participate in a caring and responsible way for the sustainability of our world.

"As part of our preparation we attended a sustainable development course within the county that covered both how to teach about SD, and how to develop a sustainable action plan for the school. We are now developing our action plan (see p. 65) and in a few months will return for a follow-up course to share with others how things have gone. In addition to the course, the networking, getting to know who can be approached for various things (e.g. fund raising), and information gathering was an essential phase in laying a good foundation on which to proceed.

Other things we have done, or intend to do, include: writing an application to the North Devon Sustainable Development Fund; writing to companies to ask them to sponsor or donate outdoor clothing; targeting local garden centres to seek their involvement (donation of seeds, tools, etc.); developing a community plot of land for growing vegetables and fruit; and embedding use of outdoor areas into the curriculum so that the outdoor space becomes a key resource in care for self, others and environment. We recognise that, realistically, this is a three-year programme! To achieve the goals, long-term training with all staff and involvement of pupils through the school council will be an important part of future plans."

FOOD aND FarminG

Food for thought

The purpose of this activity from Edwalton Primary School in Nottinghamshire was to encourage pupils to start thinking about the processes that keep a farm working and to begin to appreciate the hard work and different people required to run a farm.

Key ESD concepts

- citizenship and stewardship
- diversity
- sustainable change
- uncertainty and precaution

Subject links

- geography
- science
- PSHCE: community support and people who help us

Other links

ECM 1: Be healthy
ECM 3: Enjoy and achieve
ECM 4: Make a positive contribution to society
ECM 5: Achieve economic well-being
SEAL: Pupils gain emotionally, intellectually and physically; they develop emotional attachment to their farm which increases their levels of environmental concern.

Planned outcomes

- Citizenship and stewardship: knowledge that animals and crops need to be cared for if a farm is to be successful.
- Diversity: some understanding of the components needed for a successful farming environment.
- Sustainable change: developing awareness of current and future roles we might have as a community in relation to sustainable farming.
- Uncertainty and precaution: ability to think about different 'what if?' scenarios and solutions, e.g. if animals become sick, the weather is especially bad, etc.

Other geography outcomes

- Development of relevant farm and landscape vocabulary.
- Some recognition of how the farm has become the way it is and how it might change.
- Fieldwork investigations outside of the classroom.
- Growing ability to describe what a place (the farm) is like and the jobs that people do to sustain it.

Essential resources

- Ideally, a local farm who will allow visits and/or send a representative (possibly with animals and/or items of food) to visit the school.
- Good quality photographs and video resources.
- Access to relevant websites.

Starting points

Edwalton Primary School in Nottinghamshire is lucky enough to have a small farm on the premises, and although this is not something that every school can have, the enquiry questions asked show how pupils can begin to think about the many related aspects of farming practice in relation to our own lives.

Teacher Jane Whittle explained how pupils began by talking about what they already knew about farming practice, using a photograph of one of the animals as a stimulus.

> I showed pupils a picture of Molly as a lamb and asked 'Who is this?'. Through our ensuing discussion they soon realised that Molly the sheep is actually older than they are and that she was born and raised on the farm. We then went on to discuss the benefits of our farm from Molly's perspective (e.g. a new stable, the nicely painted fences, lots of food, her friends, e.g. the goats, and the care she gets from pupils).
>
> I used photographs to show pupils that the farm has been here for 50 years. I then asked them to think about who has helped to keep the farm going for all this time and they drew their ideas on a big sheet of paper. Through questions, I helped pupils to identify people they might not immediately think of, such as the vet (health and safety aspect of animal welfare) and the company that buys our hay (enterprise and economic aspects of the farm).

These pupils engaged with this activity from the outset because the starting point was something that they were familiar with, which was also a good way to prompt further thinking.

Prompt questions

- Who is this?
- What do we know about this animal?
- What do we know about her life?
- Who helps to look after her (and the rest of the farm)?
- How do they help?
- What does Molly eat?
- Where does she live?
- Where does her food come from?
- Who pays for it?
- Who looks after her if she gets ill?
- How could we find out?
- What other questions could we ask?
- Who should we ask?

Activities and challenges

Interviewing others

Pupils thought of a question to ask a key member of the school and, using a small hand-held digital movie camera, worked together to carry out interviews. It is also useful if an adult can scribe some of the responses as well. The videos were then downloaded for pupils to watch and discuss. Jane explained that she made this activity even more fun by getting pupils to interview some of the animals as well:

> Our pupils interviewed the pigs, asking them if they enjoyed living on the farm and who helps to keep it going. A plastic microphone was used to make it look like a real interview. I just hope one of your pupils understands OINK!

Jobs on the farm

After identifying the jobs already done by other people, discussion groups were set up for the pupils to think about the jobs that they could do on the farm. Pupils were also asked to think about the animals already kept on the farm and whether any other animals might be needed and why. As a final activity, pupils were challenged to give their view of the future of the farm by drawing and talking about what things they would change and why.

Using secondary sources

The FACE Food and Farming pack has a range of good quality images and video clips to stimulate similar activities for those

Caring for our World **Food and Farming**

schools who do not have access to a real farm. Pupils can identify what they already know about a particular type of farming and then decide questions to ask others. Alternatively you could start pupils thinking about farming by examining items of food that they are particularly familiar with, such as a loaf of bread, a pint of milk or a fruit such as apples, and getting pupils to say what they already know about them and what they would like to know. Recording pupils' ideas and responses at this stage can be a useful aid to assessment.

Making global links
Food is a topic that all pupils can relate to in their everyday lives, and thinking about where our food comes from, how it gets here and why can provide lots of opportunities to link local and global perspectives. Investigating the contents of a shopping bag will reveal a wide range of countries of origin. Is it always better to buy locally-produced food though? Some overseas farmers depend on selling their produce abroad in order to make a living so the answers are not always straightforward.

Challenges for pupils

Some pupils lack confidence in speaking and so an activity built around this can seem daunting for them. Jane explained some of the challenges associated with her interviewing activity:

> " Talking to key members of the school on a specific topic proved difficult for some younger members of the class who lacked confidence – although everyone was willing to use the camera! To overcome this pupils were divided into groups of varied dynamics to allow for peer support. Timing was also difficult as some of the pupils could have run on for hours! Adapt the activity to whatever pupils are able to deliver. "

Another challenge for pupils is thinking how they might be actively involved in the running of a farm, rather than just learning about it. These pupils are taught that they will have a real responsibility in helping to care for the animals and, over time, this helps to build real confidence.

Challenges for teachers

Language and communication
Developing appropriate language to enable younger pupils to convey their ideas is always challenging for teachers. Pupils should have lots of opportunities to talk about, share and extend ideas by practising new words in relevant contexts. New vocabulary is best learnt in association with first-hand experiences, and although not all pupils can access a real farm, materials such as hay, wheat and corn, can be brought into the classroom, and model farms, buildings and vehicles can be used in miniature play.

Talking or drawing are often more suitable for younger pupils but it can be a challenge to find the most effective ways to collect pupils' ideas and also to ask the right kinds of questions. Jane noted that:

> " A worksheet asking pupils to list people who help on the farm did not satisfy the discussion we had. The pupils wanted to make reference to the rain and sun that makes the food that the animals eat grow as a key aspect of sustaining the farm but the sheet did not reflect this idea. For key stage one pupils, therefore, I would adapt the sheet to ask 'what keeps our farm going and going?'. "

Animal welfare
Discussing where our food comes from with young pupils can get problematic when it comes to discussing how animals are reared for their meat. Handling this aspect of farming so that pupils access truthful information whilst not becoming upset is a real challenge for teachers and involves a careful selection of accurate information to give a balanced view of the facts if prompted by pupil questions. Thinking about the three underpinning principles of ESD – economic, social and environmental – can help teachers present different perspectives about farming practices.

Global links
It is also important to present a balanced view when discussing where our food comes from. Local food may have the advantage in terms of supporting local communities, reducing food miles and being fresher, but some overseas communities rely on exports to make a living. There may also be more carbon emissions from practices needed to grow some foods in colder climates such as ours so identifying best practice can be complex. It is therefore unhelpful to make blanket generalisations, rather we should query who benefits, why and how?

Vocabulary
Animal names, vet, environment, crops, hay, field, shelter, barn, food, farming year, landscape, boundary.

Future perspectives

Food is one of our most basic needs and identifying where and how our needs can be met in the future is a very real and relevant issue. In this particular example, pupils talked about what they could do now and what their future role would be – actively developing more responsibility for animal care. They also had the role models of older pupils in the school who already had responsibility for looking after the animals so they could envisage their own future roles. It is important that the pupils were able to identify that the farm was only sustained through ongoing action. The uncertainty and precaution element of ESD can be well illustrated in a food and farming context through discussion of 'what if' scenarios, e.g. what happens if the weather is especially wet at harvest? What if the animals become sick?

This discussion (right) reveals how these pupils are actively collaborating to problem solve and are learning to make real decisions. It's evident that the pupils are totally engaged and feel that they have a key responsibility.

Teacher reflections

Jane explained how pupils coped with the activities and how their responses helped her to gauge their knowledge and understanding:

> " Pupils asked, unprompted, to write a thank you letter to the staff at school who helped to look after the farm. This revealed that they had understood the concept of support from different people. Pupils were able to suggest a wide range of reasons why Molly the sheep likes to live on the farm, including her new fence, the grass and her friends the goats, as well as the people who come to see her.
>
> Discussing how shops keep the farm going by providing us with hay led to an interesting discussion of how God and the world must also help – the beginnings of global sustainability from a four-year-old! This also prompted the issue of rain and growing vegetables and gave an opportunity for pupils to think further afield than the school grounds. Pupils were aghast when I asked if food arrived by magic and could easily explain the basic principles behind food production, thus providing further assessment of their knowledge and understanding. "

Pupils' voices

Jane recalled a discussion pupils had on the topic of 'other animals we could have':

> " It was interesting that when the pupils were asked what other animals they would like on the farm, they suggested chickens but only if there were no foxes. This idea came from one pupil who had seen something about foxes attacking chickens on the news and led into a discussion about the sustainability of the farm animals in terms of aspects we had less control over. "

I would like to have chickens on our farm.

But I saw on the television that foxes kill chickens.

Why do foxes kill chickens?

They like to eat them all up.

Then I would like chickens with no foxes.

Yes, we want the chickens to be safe.

Will they eat other animals?

We'll put a big fence up!

But they might come in the middle of the night.

Well should we have chickens then?

People who help to keep the farm going are.....

hEDE

Arrange a visit to a local shop or supermarket and ask if you can interview the produce manager about where they source their produce from. Due to customer demand some of the major supermarkets are now selling much more local produce. Understanding that we have some power as consumers to influence decisions like this is an important lesson for pupils.

Assessment for Learning

The interviewing activity culminated in a replay of the films and a discussion about the information that had been collected. This was a good opportunity for pupils to reflect on what they had learnt and how they might improve their understanding. It also gave teachers ample opportunity to challenge any continuing misconceptions. The drawing and writing activities provided evidence of pupils' understanding, and although the initial discussion had taken place in a group, each piece of work was individual and provided valid formative assessment.

Why we chose this

The benefits of having a farm on the premises are enormous but impractical for many schools. However, this example demonstrates excellent use of an enquiry process that starts by building on what pupils already know and want to know about their everyday lives. This captures pupils' innate curiosity and enthusiasm for the world around them and this is an approach that can be easily replicated.

Further ideas

As previously discussed, using a starting point such as a lamb or an item of food to engage the pupils in an enquiry is a process that can be easily replicated. Ask a local farmer to visit the school and, if possible, to bring some animals in and to answer questions that pupils have devised beforehand.

Questioning can be difficult for young pupils so using contexts that develop this skill are especially useful. For example, take an apple and brainstorm with pupils a list of questions that they could ask about it.

Use pictures of farming landscapes to discuss: boundaries and what they might be for; how farming has changed the landscape and why; which landscapes pupils prefer and why; familiar and non-familiar landscape features; different aspects of the farming year, etc. The FACE farming pack also has a range of activities with good quality images to support them.

Older pupils might like to investigate some of the blogs written by farmers' children on the 'Connect Kids' website (*www.kidsconnectcampaign.co.uk/*).

References and further resources

Pupil books

Browne, E. (2003) *Handa's Hen*. London: Walker Books.

Chamberlin, M. and Chamberlin, R. (2006) *Mama Panya's Pancakes: A village tale from Kenya*. Bath: Barefoot Books.

French, V. and Bartlett, A. (1995) *Oliver's Vegetables*. London: Hodder Children's Books. (home focus)

French, V. and Bartlett, A. (1998) *Oliver's Fruit Salad*. London: Hodder Children's Books. (global scale)

French, V. and Bartlett, A. (2000) *Oliver's Milkshake*. London: Hodder Children's Books. (local focus)

Websites

www.kidsconnectcampaign.co.uk/
The Farmer's Weekly Kids Connect Campaign website has some useful links and information about school trips to farms. It also has a 'farming heroes for kids' section which highlights different issues, e.g. food miles. Really interesting is the 'Kids Connect' blog where children from farming communities speak about their everyday lives – good reading and thinking prompts for upper KS2.

www.face-online.org.uk
The Food and Countryside Education website. Partners include many big names from the crops and farming lobby as well as a diverse mix of other farm-related organisations. A useful site with many free resources and links, as well as an image gallery.

www.soilassociation.org/
The Soil Association is the UK's leading campaigning and certification organisation for organic food and farming.

farming links

At Johnstown Primary School in Carmarthenshire, the curricular work has encouraged pupils to forge strong links with local farmers. Recent highlights have included a visit by a pig, and another by a lamb who became the pupils' responsibility for the day. This involved regular bottle-feeding sessions and checks to make sure it hadn't escaped! Such first-hand experience and responsibility are vital precursors to developing principles of care for oneself, others and the environment, and gives young pupils a great deal of motivation and satisfaction.

A less exciting but equally successful project followed a visit from a local farmer who challenged the pupils to grow their own potato crop. The farmer gave the pupils the seed potatoes to start them off and kept in touch with them throughout the growing period using the internet. The pupils sent back images of the crop's progress and were able to gain feedback about any problems they encountered or queries they had. This kind of direct collaboration with community experts makes learning real for pupils.

putting the child and community first

Pupils, school and community are at the heart of Yeo Valley Primary School's approach to sustainable development. Headteacher Jan Reid decided that there was no point studying sustainability if the school and community were not taking a sustainable approach to the pupils' education. Staff, parents and governors have therefore worked together to identify which social, environmental and economic elements of the school and curriculum were already supporting pupils' education about sustainable development, and which needed looking at.

Yeo Valley has the philosophy of 'teach the child' rather than 'teach the subject'. This puts pupils and their education at the heart of any decisions that are made about how the school develops. Their approach to ESD is therefore focused on about solar panels, wind turbines and energy monitors. Instead it is about creating a school and classroom atmosphere that makes pupils want to come to school and learn each day. This means thinking about the social as well as the physical environment. Examples of the initial changes include:

- Cloakrooms being removed from corridors in order to provide free, uncluttered space to move around
- The relocation of a corridor that passed through two classrooms so that the classrooms had their own, uninterrupted space
- KS1 classrooms now opening directly onto a terraced area with sand and water trays
- The relocation of the Reception classroom closer to the nursery so that the two classes can work together
- Development of the grounds to create increased opportunities for outdoor learning.

These physical changes have a huge impact on the social dynamic of the school as they have helped create the right sort of atmosphere in which care for self, others and the environment can flourish.

Now this has been established, the school is looking at more school and community linked developments, such as:

- The 'Grab a Bag' scheme where each week a local farm sells a bag of their vegetables and a recipe for £1 at school. This is very successful in encouraging parents and pupils to cook with fresh local produce, and has led to follow-up work in the classroom about carbon responsibilities. At its peak, 80 bags were being sold each week.
- In conjunction, the school tuck shop now sells only healthy foods such as fruit portions and carrot sticks. This has had huge impact on pupils' behaviour and their attitudes to healthy lifestyles. They now do not eat anything other than fruit for break times.
- The global dimension has been introduced through a 'Food for Thought' programme with a link school in Uganda. Pupils in both schools exchange ideas and gain a range of

alternative perspectives on aspects of their learning.

- The Governors now provide a yearly grant to each pupil to ensure that all are able to take part in educational visits.
- The SEAL programme is now embedded throughout the school.
- An organic garden has been established, with each class taking turns to work in the garden. The produce is used in the school kitchens. Water for the garden is collected in a water butt. Classes relate what they do in the garden to learning in the classroom.
- Pupils are involved in designing a pond area.
- The School Council has representatives from each class and ensures that pupils have a say about their school.

The strength of this relationship between curriculum, campus and community can be seen in the following example.

Two years ago the school was looking to build a room where staff could work with parents towards raising the standards of the pupils. Since then, the wider community group has become involved and the plans have developed into a centre for families and the local community. The pupils at Yeo Valley have been part of the development process: devising questionnaires, taking part in planning exercises and talking to the community about their needs and visions. The proposal is now for three multi-use games areas with facilities and changing rooms, and £3 million community centre. At present the local authority and county councillors are conducting a feasibility study but everyone is committed to ensuring that both phases are completed as soon as possible. The centre will benefit a hugely deprived area and ensure that the work of the agencies, such as Sure Start, social services and the local government, and the school will be sustained in the future.

healthy citizenship

Eastchurch Primary School have a permanent Green Flag award, which is testimony to their long commitment to the Eco-Schools principles and their own regularly reviewed policy for sustainable development. The school also holds Healthy Schools status and believes it is very important to develop and model healthy living ideals with their pupils.

Only fruit is now allowed for break-time snacks, and playground monitors collect and compost the waste each day. The School Council has representatives from each year group and part of their job is to liaise regularly with the kitchen staff about their school meals. One of the big successes was in prompting the school kitchen to source more produce locally.

The pupils enjoy being able to work in the grounds at lunchtime and in after-school clubs to grow produce – mainly salad items and herbs – which are used in the school kitchen during the summer months. Pupils also grow organic potatoes, greens and onions which they sell to make money for more gardening equipment.

The school has a range of curricular opportunities that support ESD including:
- cooking and tasting different foods, from both their own and other countries.
- devising healthy lunchboxes and school meals.
- designing a healthy sandwich (which is then eaten on a short outing) with environmentally-friendly packaging.

- visiting local shops and farms on field trips. Pupils have the opportunity to devise their own questions before the visit and gain understanding through first-hand experiences.

FOreSt SchOOl

Learning naturally

This example from Winkleigh Primary School, Devon, shows what a forest school is and how such an approach to learning in the outdoors can develop pupils' understanding of the natural world and their relationship with it.

Key ESD concepts

- interdependence
- citizenship and stewardship
- diversity
- quality of life

Subject links

- science
- geography
- literacy
- maths
- art

Other links

ECM 1: Be healthy
ECM 2: Stay safe
ECM 3: Enjoy and achieve
SEAL: Forest School has a strong emphasis on social and emotional learning in the context of natural environments.
Personalised Learning: A guiding principle of Forest School is that it uses pupils' interests as a starting point for learning.

Planned outcomes

- Interdependence: understanding of the woodland environment and how all elements within it are interrelated; awareness of humans' impact on the environment.
- Citizenship and stewardship: development of social skills; greater confidence in own abilities; increased trust between pupils and practitioners.
- Diversity: increased awareness and knowledge of woodland flora and fauna; respect for the natural environment; ability to identify what does and doesn't belong in the woodland environment.
- Quality of life: understanding risks and knowing how to cope with them; greater understanding of waste and the need to conserve resources; a responsible attitude towards the use of woodland resources.

Other geography outcomes

- skills in route finding (journey sticks, follow my leader)
- a sense of the woodland as a place
- consideration of suitable locations for shelters, campfire, etc.

Essential resources

- a natural outdoor environment, preferably wooded, large enough to give pupils freedom to explore and be out of sight of each other and adults for short periods of time, but with a secure perimeter for safety.
- time for regular, weekly visits
- Wellington boots and waterproof coats and trousers for every pupil (a class set of these is well worth the investment).
- parent helpers: with younger pupils the adult–child ratio is preferably 1:4.

Starting points

For teachers

Forest School, if it is to be done properly, requires a qualified Forest School Leader. Often this is someone from a local environmental or Forest School centre (a list of these can be found on the Forest Education website), but many schools also invest in Level 1 training for selected teachers and teaching assistants.

An important point to note is that while Forest School takes place in natural outdoor environments, it is not another name for outdoor education. It has its own guiding principles that distinguish it from other approaches and, as Jenny Doyle, Forest School Co-ordinator in Worcestershire, says:

> What makes the Forest School unique is its emphasis on pupils learning outside the traditional classroom and having the freedom to explore the ever-changing environment, to take risks and 'assess risks for themselves'. Forest School is also a continuum, not a one-off trip: pupils visit for a minimum of one session per week throughout the year (Doyle, 2006 p. 18).

Murray and O'Brien (2006) have summarised the key features of Forest School as:

- the use of a woodland, and therefore 'wild', setting
- learning that is responsive to pupils' interests but that can be linked to the national curriculum
- the freedom to explore using multiple senses
- regular visits over a significant period of time
- a low adult-to-pupil ratio.

However, while each Forest School will have similar guiding principles, they will differ according to the available environment, the age, social and cultural backgrounds of the pupils and the interests of the Forest School leader. For example, at Winkleigh Primary School, classes are divided into two so that groups are of a manageable size (about 15 pupils). Rather than visit the Forest School site once a week for the whole year, each group has one full day once a fortnight for a ten-week period: Reception in the Summer term and year 3 in the Autumn term.

For pupils

Teacher Naomi Alexander explains how:

> "On the first visit, it is important to introduce pupils to the woodland area and explain how each visit will be structured. In some respects the visits will be quite repetitive, but the familiarity of the routine and repetition of activities gives the pupils a secure environment in which to gradually challenge themselves and learn how to take risks.
>
> At Winkleigh Primary School the starting point is Forest School Values – an ethos of looking after self, others and our environment. When pupils arrive for their first visit they follow an arrow trail (made with sticks from the wood) to find the camp, taking it in turn to be leaders, then carrying out a series of activities, interspersed with discussions around the camp fire area, that introduce them to the Forest School Values. During the next visit they are invited to lay trails for each other to find hidden objects, for example, a teddy. At the beginning of each visit orientation time – 'feeling' themselves back in the woodland – is used to ensure that pupils make the most of the day."

Prompt questions

Reflecting on the arrow trail:

- how easy was it to find the camp?
- what made it easy?
- what did you notice on your way to the camp?
- what did you see/hear/feel?

Sitting on logs around the camp fire:

- what can you see (when you look up/down)?
- sit very quietly. What can you hear?
- close your eyes. Now what can you hear?
- can you tell where the sound is coming from?

Activities

As noted above, a key principle of Forest School is that pupils have the freedom to explore using all their senses. Many of the activities are therefore responsive to the pupils' observations and interests, and these will vary according to the time of year, the weather on the day of the visit, and the focus for learning on the previous visit. However, some structure to each visit is also needed and this can be provided by planned activities such as those suggested below.

Un-nature trail

This activity helps pupils to develop an understanding of the term 'natural'. Beforehand, you will need to distribute a variety of objects in the woodland that are not usually found there. Introduce the game by asking pupils what things can usually be found in the woodland. Then explain that you have hidden a number of things that don't belong – can they find them? This activity can be carried out individually or in pairs (increasing co-operation and sharing skills) and you should ensure there are plenty of objects to be found so that everyone has a chance of success. Objects are brought back to the campfire where a discussion can be held about what natural and unnatural mean. This can lead to a discussion of rubbish in the woodland (some of the objects brought back may be ones that you did not hide!) and what should be done with it. It is also a great way to assess observation skills.

Making fire

The campfire is a central focus for any Forest School. As time progresses, and under the careful direction of the Forest School leader, pupils will learn to start the fire (without matches) themselves. Until that time, all can be involved in gathering

the materials required to start the fire. Ask each pupil to bring back the smallest twig they can find. Before these are placed on the campfire they can be compared until the smallest twig is identified. This provides opportunities for discussions about size – which is thinnest? shortest? Are they all twigs? Then ask pupils to bring back a stick, ensuring that they understand that only sticks from the woodland floor should be gathered. What is the difference between a stick and a twig? Explain to pupils that they should only gather dry twigs and sticks and why. Where are the damp/dry ones (this will alter depending on the weather).

Let's eat!
For this activity you will need flour, bottles of water, mixing bowls and some long sticks to hold over the fire. Divide pupils into groups, each with their own set of equipment. Explain that they need to mix enough water into the flour to turn it into a dough that is sticky enough to cling to the end of the long sticks. When this is ready, the dough should be divided into portions, one for each person in the group. Each pupil takes their portion, rolls it into a sausage shape, winds it around the end of their stick, and holds it over the fire to cook. Taking turns will be important here! The dough needs to be held close enough to the embers of the fire to cook, but not so close that it will burn. This will be a question of trial and error. Remove the bread from the fire and tap to see if it is ready (the bread is cooked when there is

a hollow sound). Let it cool down then eat! Afterwards, discuss appreciating food we make for ourselves and ideas about waste: did all the bread get eaten? Did some groups use more water than was needed? What will happen to the waste? Safety around the fire is another important area to discuss: what did pupils find made the cooking safer – distance from fire, length of cooking stick, width of cooking stick, weight of cooking stick, steady hand …

Challenges

Challenges for pupils
Challenges are inherent in all the activities above. They are organised in such a way that there are both personal and group challenges that are physical, emotional, social and intellectual.
- Physical: negotiating routes around the woodland; climbing; judging what is safe and what risks can be taken.
- Emotional: overcoming fear of falling and of fire; providing emotional support for each other; coping with all weathers.
- Social: working as an individual for a collective product; skills in taking turns; cooking and eating together.
- Intellectual: distinguishing between natural and 'un-natural' features of woodland; making a dough of the correct consistency; properties of materials; mathematical challenges.

Challenges for teachers

> " We have been doing Forest School for six years. Getting started required careful preparation: thinking about where funds would come from for wet weather clothing so that all pupils could take part no matter what their personal circumstances, ensuring that there were enough adult helpers, and finding the right place for the Forest experience. We have used three different woodland areas in the last six years, and have now settled on one that is owned by a parent and only two miles away from the school thus reducing time and transport costs. "

Challenges for parents
In many Forest School activities there are safety issues that need to be considered. As already mentioned, central to Forest School is the pupil-centred approach to risk and risk taking and, with careful guidance from the Forest School leader, pupils learn to take risks and assess risks for themselves. In our health and safety conscious society this can pose a real challenge to parents who may not appreciate the nature of the risks or the approach to these.

> " At Winkley, our solution is to involve parents as much as possible by:
>
> - Holding a parents' meeting at the beginning of each term or year
>
> (an example of how such a meeting is run is provided by Hope School on their website – see p. 34)
>
> - Encouraging parents to become volunteers so they can see for themselves what is involved. "

Vocabulary

Woodland, forest, trail, nature, natural, unnatural, waste, fire, spark, embers, safe, risk, cook, dough, names of plants and animals specific to your area

Pupils' voices

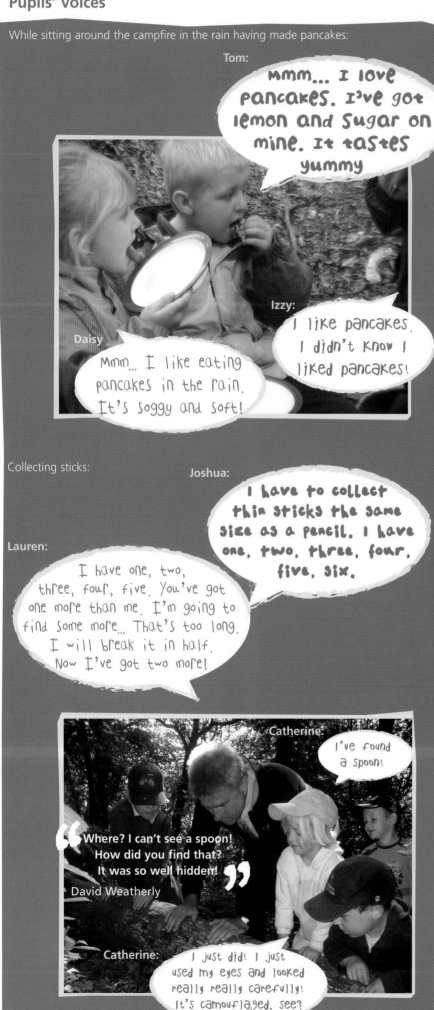

While sitting around the campfire in the rain having made pancakes:

Tom:

mmm... I love pancakes. I've got lemon and sugar on mine. It tastes yummy

Izzy:

I like pancakes. I didn't know I liked pancakes!

Daisy

Mmm... I like eating pancakes in the rain. It's soggy and soft!

Collecting sticks:

Joshua:

I have to collect thin sticks the same size as a pencil. I have one, two, three, four, five, six.

Lauren:

I have one, two, three, four, five. You've got one more than me. I'm going to find some more... That's too long. I will break it in half. Now I've got two more!

Catherine:

I've found a spoon!

Where? I can't see a spoon! How did you find that? It was so well hidden!
David Weatherly

Catherine:

I just did! I just used my eyes and looked really really carefully! It's camouflaged, see?

Teacher reflections

" We are constantly surprised by how pupils react to Forest School and what they learn from it. It offers those who might not usually perform well in the classroom a chance to shine. They grow enormously in confidence and social skills, and their growing regard and affection for self, others and their environment is evident for all to see. We have noticed that some farmers' children find it quite difficult to connect to the National Curriculum but thrive in this environment. Some boys with special educational needs in our school have also blossomed.

As far a ESD is concerned, when working with the Reception class it is not usually possible to say whether the pupils are consciously aware of how what they are learning links to sustainable development. However, our pupils visit Forest School in Reception and year 3 and this has been the case for six years. Those who had the experience in Reception are now revisiting in year 3. We have been astounded at how much they have remembered from their earlier experiences. We firmly believe that these experiences are so memorable that they provide a lasting foundation for the more explicit learning that will come in upper KS2 and at KS3. "

Futures perspectives

" Any woodland area used for Forest School has to be carefully managed so that it is not degraded by the use that is made of it. We rotate sites so that over the course of a year or two each has the chance to regenerate. It is a question of balancing rights and responsibilities – pupils have a right to outdoor education, but there is also a responsibility to the environment that is a home for a variety of plants and animals. If diversity is to be maintained then rotation is an essential part of Forest School.

This type of thinking is developed more explicitly with Reception pupils who learn to balance needs and wants, for example, that they should never use more wood for the fire than they need because the woodland animals also need it as part of their habitat and to survive. "

Further ideas

Learning that takes place in Forest School should not be seen as separate from that which happens in the classroom during the rest of the week. It is vital that pupils are able to make connections between the two if learning is to be transferred.

Global dimension and sustainability

We also have a link with a school in The Gambia. A Gambian teacher came to our school and saw the amount of waste that is produced at mealtimes. As a result of this we have chosen to focus on environmental issues in both schools, exchanging information and learning from each other about how we can be more sustainable.

As we followed the arrow trail of sticks or stones in Forest School, Fran said 'Do you know that people all over the world make trails like this?'. When Fran forgot her fork to eat her pasta salad she made some chopsticks and told pupils that people in other countries don't always use a fork or spoon and that many people eat food with their hands.

We use charcoal from the camp fire to draw with in school, take biodegradable waste from picnic lunches back to put in the school compost bin, and are sparse with water when, for example, cooking and washing. We feel that by modelling such behaviours we are encouraging pupils to recognise what positive actions they can take to look after the environment.

Michael observed:

We must remember to take our apple cores and banana skins back to school for composting. We don't want apple trees growing in this wood. It's the wrong place!

Assessment for Learning

Time for reflection and evaluation at the end of each Forest School day is needed to ensure the learning is understood. We do a 'buzz' session at the end of each visit where pupils sit around the campfire and take it in turns to say something that they have enjoyed, learned or found hard that day. Turns do not follow around the circle. Instead pupils are encouraged to wait for a gap in the conversation before saying something. If two people speak at once they decide who will go first.

Storytelling (part of our shared global project)

Fran now tells a story at most sessions and pupils are learning to re-tell them. At Forest School they make puppets, dramatise by sequencing the story and co-operate as a group.

When such reflections are carried out on a regular basis the Forest School leader and teachers will, through their ongoing observations of pupils during the days and weeks, be able to tailor their questions to particular pupils and build up a picture of how they are developing over time. Each week's information is useful for planning the following week's activities. You will have some idea from your observations, but asking pupils for their points of view can sometimes surprise you!

Using the language of learning

We talk a lot about learning – about what and how we learn – so that pupils know what an 'active learner' is and begin to develop an understanding of their responsibility in the process of learning. At the end of the ten weeks I talk to the pupils individually and scribe a mind map for them with photos asking 'What did you like?', 'How did you feel?', 'What did you learn?' and 'How did you learn?'

Tom: I thought people singing and eating their lunch was fun

Ella: I learnt to look carefully when I was finding objects

Connor: I learnt using my eyes and ears, and I share ideas and link things

Harry: I felt happy when I was collecting tiny things to put in Fran's Smartie box because I was the only one doing it

Why we chose this

Anyone who has taken part in Forest School sees at first hand what a difference being in the natural environment can make to pupils' learning. The concept of care for self, others and the environment is at the heart of this approach, as is a deep understanding of the concepts of diversity and interdependence.

References and further resources

Articles
Doyle, J. (2006) 'If you go down to the woods today', *Primary Geographer,* 59, pp. 17-19.

Books
Murray, R. and O'Brien, L. (2006) *A Marvellous Opportunity for Children to Learn: A participatory evaluation of Forest School in England and Wales.* Norwich: HMSO.

Websites
www.forestschools.com/earlyyears.php
Some ideas specifically for Early Years, but the site itself also very useful with training packs and other downloadable materials.

www.foresteducation.org/forest_schools.php
Resources to download and a very useful county directory so you can find where there are Forest Schools near you.

http://hopeblog.ethink.org.uk/category/class-1/forest-schools/
Hope School's website. Includes a PowerPoint presentation that is used with parents to explain the principles and purposes of Forest School. There are also two audio-blogs giving pupils' perspectives of Forest School.

www.shropshire.gov.uk/forestschools.nsf
Downloadable resources are available by following the 'activity resources' link.

---

string trails

Jane Whittle from Edwalton Primary School describes a simple, fun activity to support young pupils learning simple navigation skills.

Resources
- Very large ball of string
- *Titch Out and About* (Pat Hutchins, 2000, Red Fox)

This deceptively simple activity encourages teamwork and gives young pupils lots of confidence. In finding their way back safely, pupils have to consider both care for themselves and their environment and have the opportunity for observing the environment at first hand. It is an example of successful planning across campus and curriculum.

> " The class went out into the woods and sat on the logs in the outdoor classroom. The pupils were then read the story *Titch Out and About.* Titch and his brother and sister go for a walk while staying at Granddad's house but they get lost. Luckily Titch saves the day by following a thread that has unravelled from his scarf to find the way back.
>
> Pupils then followed a trail of string already wound through the woods, over, under and round obstacles. When they reached the end they were told they were lost! They then worked out that by following the string the other way, then like Titch they could find their way back! "

Forest School or beach School?

> " At Appledore Primary School our medium term plans are worked around Oxfam's Global Citizenship concepts (see below) and the SEAL programme. We feel that there is a good overlap between these and ESD and that the concepts are addressed through them. "

The key elements for responsible Global Citizenship

Knowledge and understanding
- Social justice and equity
- Diversity
- Globalisation and interdependence
- Sustainable development
- Peace and conflict

Skills
- Critical thinking
- Ability to argue effectively
- Ability to challenge injustice and inequalities
- Respect for people and things
- Co-operation and conflict resolution

Values and attitudes
- Sense of identity and self-esteem
- Empathy
- Commitments to social justic and equity
- Value and respect for diversity
- Concern for the environment and commitment to sustainable development
- Belief that people can make a difference

This material is taken from Education for Global Citizenship: A Guide for Schools (2006), with permission of Oxfam GB, Oxfam House, John Smith Drive, Cowley, Oxford OX4 2JY, UK www.oxfam.org.uk/education. Oxfam GB does not necessarily endorse any text or activities that accompany the material.

> We believe that fieldwork, or outdoor learning, should be a part of every topic and currently ensure this through Forest School. Each class has a term of Forest School experience every year. We are now thinking about how we might turn this into a 'Beach School' experience since this environment is on the pupils' doorstep and readily accessible.
>
> The concepts, skills and attitudes of Global Citizenship (Oxfam, 2006) are embedded through our units of work. We like to use a more cross-curricular way of working and the humanities seem the natural lead for this work. For example, year 1 begin by doing a number of small topics lasting between one and eight weeks that focus on themselves, growing up, animals and their young and toys. Through this pupils learn about the world around them and develop caring attitudes towards themselves and others. Later in the year this moves on to a unit of work about the seaside, which has a strong fieldwork component and focuses on caring for their environment now and for the future. In year 2 there is a unit about Chembakolli in which pupils develop their understanding of diversity and how to use the world's resources carefully.

An example of Appledore's approach to medium-term planning can be found on pages 63-4.

Sally Squirrel circle time

Shropshire Education Advisory Service have devised many Forest School activities, some of which are available online at *www.shropshire.gov.uk/forestschools.nsf*. They advocate the use of Sally Squirrel circle time at the end of the day to help pupils to reflect on what they have learnt.

Example 1

Sally Squirrel (a glove puppet) asks pupils about their experiences using such questions as:
• Did anything make you laugh today?
• Did you feel proud of anything you did today?
• Did anybody help you to do something today?
• Did you feel unhappy about doing anything today?
• Did you try something new today?
• Have you learned anything new about someone else?

Example 2

Sally Squirrel provides different sentences for individuals to complete around the circle, such as:
• I liked it when…
• I worked with someone else to…
• I was helped by…
• It was difficult to…
• Nobody listened when…
• I've learned that…
• I surprised myself when…
• I felt unhappy when…

school Grounds

Grounds for action

This example shows how even very young pupils can be actively involved in designing and developing their school grounds.

Key ESD concepts

- citizenship and stewardship
- interdependence
- diversity
- sustainable change
- uncertainty and precaution

Subject links

- knowledge and understanding of the world
- language development
- mathematics
- citizenship

Other links

ECM 3: Enjoy and achieve
ECM 4: Make a positive contribution
ECM 5: Achieve economic well-being
SEAL: Pupils develop emotional responses to place, and value them and the work they have done to help shape them.
Personalised Learning: Pupils develop aspects of self-identity through engagement and responsibility that builds on their strengths and interests.

Planned outcomes

- Citizenship and stewardship: growing responsibility for the school grounds and ability to take suitable actions.
- Interdependence: knowing that what we do can affect other living things and the places they live.
- Diversity: increased knowledge of flora and fauna in the school grounds and of how we can protect them; increased respect for a range of views and opinions.
- Sustainable change: growing understanding of how our actions in the school grounds can affect changes for better or for worse.
- Uncertainty and precaution: developing awareness of the possible roles of parents and the community in helping to look after the school grounds; growing confidence in everyday problem-solving abilities.

Other geography outcomes:

- developing skills in asking geographical questions
- developing sense of place and use of appropriate descriptive language; increased observational and recording skills
- growing ability to comment on where and why things are sited where they are
- growing ability to express own views about the environment
- ability to communicate views and ideas in a range of ways
- increased skill in using and making simple maps and plans
- development of a range of fieldwork skills.

Essential resources

- Access to the school grounds at any scale, from window boxes to large tracts of land
- Support from parents/the local community/local businesses
- Digital recording equipment (to record environmental changes)
- Aerial views of the school grounds and local area
- Maps and plans of the local area and school grounds.

Starting points

Improving the school grounds is something that any school can do at some scale, and many do this with spectacular results. However, the outcome is less important than the process when developing ESD principles. The Eco-Schools programme is particularly helpful here as it gives a useful blueprint for putting planning into action. Alternatively, an evaluation of what you have in terms of assets and areas for improvement is always a useful starting point and involves the entire school community in 'visioning' and planning. The best ideas can be worked on during an action day that also involves parents and locals. Ongoing evaluation and review should be used to keep everyone informed until it's time to start the cycle again. At the heart of the Eco-School ethos, and good practice in ESD, is the premise that pupils are central to the decision-making processes and have a real voice in the proceedings.

Johnstown Primary School

Johnstown Primary School is located in the busy county town of Carmarthen. Reception teacher Teresa Brunt explains how their school grounds have been improved over a number of years through ongoing work by pupils and the community:

> As the school Eco-Co-ordinator, I decided to allocate a different theme for action to each year group so that it would be their responsibility to lead developments in this area: Reception were allocated 'school grounds'; years 1 and 2 'water'; year 3 'waste management'; year 4 'litter'; year 5 'energy', and year 6 'healthy living and transport'. The youngest pupils definitely know what they like and dislike in the grounds and, due to the practical nature of this part of their curriculum, are also willing to put on their overalls and wellies and lend helping hands. This was also an opportunity to encourage parents to get involved with the development of the school grounds.

Over the last six years, many changes have taken place – all led by the pupils. The starting point for all projects is the same – encouraging and being receptive to pupils' ideas and building in time to explore different points of view and practicalities.

Prompt questions

Johnstown Primary School actively promotes the development of pupils' thinking skills, as Teresa explained:

> Through questioning, pupils (even the very youngest) develop crucial oracy skills, and because the pupils acknowledge the importance of what is in it for them (improved surroundings), they are very keen to share discussions about their grounds.

Questions included:

- What do you like (in the school grounds)?
- What don't you like?
- Why do/don't you like …?
- What would you change?
- What kinds of things do we need?
- What kinds of things do we want?
- How will we do it?
- Who will help?
- How much will it cost?
- Where will we do it?
- Who will look after it?

Activities and challenges

Teresa described the ongoing tradition of 'Feet on Friday' – a weekly 'walkabout' with pupils:

> Sometimes this involves walking and exploring in the locality but often it is spent 'foraging' in the school grounds. We have a special noticeboard in the classroom and each Friday after our walkabout, we put up a range of digital pictures taken by the pupils of things that interested them and these form the basis of much discussion during the following week. It's an ideal way to track and review what's happening in the outdoors and keep in touch with our locality.

Teresa explained that as the pupils became engaged with their grounds, they developed lots of ideas. These then had to be whittled down using critical thinking, until the projects that were achievable were identified and could be discussed with the School Council.

> Once possible projects have been agreed, we work with the pupils in designing, planning and costing. Some projects are quite small scale while others have involved help from parents and locals over a period of time.

Over the past years the following projects have been completed:

- A sensory garden
- A vegetable plot
- A quiet reading area
- A mini-beast hotel
- A shade garden
- Boundaries woven from willow wands
- A bike shelter and a buggy shelter
- A bird feeding station
- An orchard

Current projects include:

- A music installation made from reclaimed objects
- A multi-cultural garden
- A wildlife area
- A memorial garden
- A bath pond

Working with others

Each of these projects has involved careful design and presentation to others in the school. Although some have been specifically in the Early Years areas, some have been larger collaborative projects involving the whole school and this has meant representatives of the school council have had to jointly debate and agree what to do. Pupils have also designed posters to advertise their action days to parents and, following project completion, written thank-you letters to community helpers.

Creating and naming

One project was to create a mini-beast home. This involved pupils learning about habitats and choosing a suitable site and materials with which to make it. The materials were discarded logs from other areas of the school grounds. The pupils especially enjoyed thinking up a catchy name and creating a sign. The duly named 'Tree Trunk Hotel' was used in lots of curriculum work. Pupils enjoy creating and naming places, and these 'personal geographies' take on a lasting meaning.

detached

We saw flats.

We saw terraced houses.

cottage

Feet on Friday

We saw bungalows.

bungalow

We saw detached houses.

We saw mobile homes.

terraced

We saw caravans.

Busy as bees!

A similar project, but this time involving parents, was the construction of a bird feeding station aptly named 'Tweeties Bistro'.

Recycling and reclaiming

In a recent project, pupils collected donated pots and pans to build a music installation. Teresa explained how this involved designing the supportive structure; choosing items for their sound qualities; thinking how items could be painted to look attractive; and investigating where and how it could be sited.

In another project, pupils had wanted extra seating and had been excited to realise that timber cut down in another area of the school grounds could be used in their designs, although adult help was required to make this a reality. Some projects have needed greater funding which pupils have actively been involved in raising. Teresa was proud to acknowledge that the pupils didn't like to waste

anything; when an old bath was found on a part of the site, the pupils asked if they could turn it into a small pond.

Challenges for pupils

As with the design and maintenance of vegetable gardens (see also Food and Farming, pp. 20-7, and Growing Schools, pp. 12-19), these projects are never entirely finished and require attention all year round. This means that pupils have to be prepared to plan for sustained effort and think about care during the summer holidays. They quickly learn that partnerships with others in the community are extremely helpful. For example, parents and pupils living nearby have volunteered to help care for the grounds during long holidays.

Given a free rein pupils will come up with all sorts of extravagant ideas, only a few of which may have practical possibilities. This creative part of their thinking, where they let their imaginations loose, strive to problem solve and come up with original ideas, is very important. However, the critical process is also necessary so that pupils' original ideas can be whittled down into what can realistically be done. Teresa recalled that:

> **We have had some wonderfully creative thoughts from the very young children at the school, ranging from the creation of a zoo to the development of a theme park! This creativity should not be suppressed but embraced. Pupils are encouraged to draw and explain their imaginative ideas, leading to some lovely work in language development in the Early Years setting. Such ideas are used for discussion with the pupils e.g. the practicalities of caring for an elephant! Therefore pupils' ideas never diminish but become adapted through thought processes.**

The need to get parents, locals and/or businesses involved is another new challenge as pupils have to think how they will approach them and what they might say to persuade them to be involved. Teresa was very positive about pupil power:

> **Pupils have encouraged people and businesses in the local and wider community to become involved through letters, posters, press and radio appeals, sponsorship and fundraising for charities, etc.**

As well as these environmental (what can we do/change?) and social (who will help/benefit?) aspects, pupils also have to think about economic problems: how much will it cost and where will the money come from? These are aspects of great importance and Teresa observed that:

> **These problems/challenges which the pupils are faced with are ultimately problems they will face in their future lives. Consequently pupils are learning key life skills.**

Challenges for teachers

In these kinds of projects one of the main challenges for teachers is maintaining momentum and co-ordinating progress as they often involve a mix of pupils, parents and the local community, and sometimes

take many years to complete. Teaching pupils to understand conflicts of interest and that different groups may have differing opinions about what should be done and where things should be sited is also demanding. However, when handled sensitively this gives pupils an ideal opportunity to actively engage in real-life problem solving.

Teresa explained another major challenge:

> **Sometimes it's a challenge balancing different areas of Eco-Schools and inspiring other adults to get involved. Teachers already have a heavy work load but if you can show them it's not more work, it's easier to persuade them to get involved.**

It is also challenging (but important) to incorporate a global dimension that pupils can understand and relate to into work done in the school grounds. Teresa explained:

> **Pupils love to learn about the various cultures and traditions of people around the world. This year, after our latest environmental audit of the school grounds, the pupils wanted to develop one area to make a multi-cultural garden.**

Designing a multi-cultural garden is one very practical example of how a global dimension might be illustrated with young pupils but, of course, there are lots of different ways in which this can be achieved, for example: thinking about safeguarding biodiversity; sourcing and using resources wisely; and understanding how communities can work together to improve where they live without affecting others in distant places. These are all aspects of global citizenship.

Vocabulary

Landscape, garden, shelter, shade, site, specific flower names (e.g. daffodil, primrose, yarrow), specific tree names (e.g. oak, beech, poplar), specific animal names (e.g. squirrel, blackbird, toad, spider)

Pupils' voices

The opportunities for participation and inclusion through this approach are clear, and through discussion and questioning pupils acquire and practice using relevant outdoor vocabulary and sharing likes and dislikes (opinions). Although not evident at this school, some young pupils often have surprisingly limited vocabulary relating to outdoor features and little knowledge of how the natural world works because they tend to spend greater amounts of time indoors than out.

Teresa recalled asking pupils what they thought about trees and why we had them:

> **This discussion came from a pupil whose father had dug out some rotten trees in their garden and subsequently planted some new ones in their place. Another pupil responded:**

> We have trees to fill in holes in the ground in my garden. If we didn't have trees we would fall down the holes.

> Trees are important because without trees we would not have leaves

> **Well, why do we need leaves?**

> If we didn't have leaves there would be nowhere to sit when it's hot

> **This discussion took place on a 'green day' (when we were celebrating our success of achieving Eco-School Green Flag status). All pupils received a green apple for their hard work. When I informed my Reception class where the apple came from, pupils could be seen for days afterwards hugging the old tree in the school grounds (and still do when given apples, pears, etc. by their mums and dads at fruit time). All I can say is that this old tree is well loved!**

> **Pupils love to collect their fruit waste for composting but I have seen arguments between the youngest about whether to feed it to old Mr Composter or to the Wiggly Woo wormery. It is lovely to see such passionate recyclers!**

Teacher reflections

> **I believe that we all learn best through practical, fun, and meaningful experiences. If someone just informs us of a fact, it's put into our short-term memories and is ultimately lost. What I am trying to stress is the importance of meaningful hands-on early learning experiences which will stay with the pupils forever and give them skills they really will use.**
>
> **These young pupils can tell me what they think about their own surroundings – whether good or bad. Even at this very young age they are able to express their views because they are involved from start to finish in the processes of improvement. This instils a feeling of ownership of the project in question. For example, pupils often remind the teachers that the plants should be watered from the water butt not the tap. And the pupils will now never forget that plants need soil, sunlight and water to grow.**
>
> **These practical experiences break down pupils' fears of being wrong as everyone's ideas are discussed and all are included. It is so important to stress the wonderful array of language that flows from these activities. Pupils also bring in items from home to support their learning. Pupils as young as five have brought in, unprompted, wheelbarrow pictures from catalogues, flowering plants for planting, and even gardening gloves. Parents stress to me how keen and eager their child is to bring these items in. Ultimately this gets parents on board with what their children are learning in school.**

Futures thinking

Ongoing work in the school grounds is very futures-orientated because of the cycle of evaluation: plan, do and review. As the many projects were carried out over different time-scales, pupils were able to see the fruits of their labour in the short term and become more adept at planning for the longer term.

Further ideas

- Create a trail and make signs and information panels
- Provide additional habitats for wildlife, e.g. bird and bat boxes, bog gardens, tree planting
- Invite a local wildlife group into the school grounds to carry out a small mammal survey
- Design and site a story-telling chair or friendship stop
- Investigate the suitability of your site for renewable energy technologies (see Energy chapter, pp. 46-53).

Assessment for Learning

When pupils know what they want to do and how they will do it, they are more ready to take responsibility for their own learning and that of others. For example, on a weekly review of the outdoors pupils have the opportunity to discuss and report what they have seen and pose questions, as well as review vocabulary, understandings and any misconceptions. The use of drawing and talking to convey ensuing ideas gives an indication of where sensitive and supportive questioning is needed to scaffold growing understanding.

Why we chose this

The different scales of engagement and the sheer enthusiasm with which the Johnstown Primary School pupils are transforming their school grounds shows what can be achieved with either little or more substantial financial support. That it is the very youngest pupils who are leading the work and confidently developing so many different projects is very innovative. The changes wrought in the grounds also reflect the different aspects of ESD: social (through community involvement); environmental (through their care for living things and ongoing stewardship); and economic (through their fundraising activities).

References and further resources

DfES (2006) *Schools for the Future. Designing school grounds.* London:TSO. This is a practical guide that deals with many aspects of school grounds development and has a good reference and resource list.

Milner, A., Jewson, T. and Scoffham, S. (2004) 'Using the school locality', in Scoffham, S. (ed) *Primary Geography Handbook*. Sheffield: Geographical Association, pp. 180–93.

Primary Geographer (2006) Issue 59: Focus on Outdoor Learning.

Websites

www.eco-schools.org.uk
The UK website for Eco-Schools with many practical ideas and resources.

www.eco-schoolswales.org
The website for Eco-Schools in Wales.

www.ltl.org.uk
Learning Through Landscapes is an organisation with a great deal of experience in school grounds design, development and use, and they have many useful publications.

Young decision makers

Ammanford Infants School faced a challenge with their school grounds. Although the grounds were fairly extensive, the area consisted of nothing more than grass with a few shrubs. In addition, the ground was quite boggy and prone to becoming waterlogged. So, as Heather James, the school's Deputy Head, explained:

> **Pupils talked and drew ideas in class. There was lots of feedback and discussion about why some ideas might work and why others wouldn't. We also used this as a homework exercise to get parents involved and inputing ideas. Each class then put forward a few ideas which were displayed in the hall. The school council and the staff then voted on the designs they liked best.**

The pupils designed play frames, decking areas and a bridge to cross the wettest area. There were also ideas for sculptures, seating, and the planting of a wildlife area. An innovative approach was to not only enlist community support but to ask the Princes Trust for support. This was granted in the form of a week's worth of donated labour. The project is still ongoing, with a great deal of local community support, and Heather explained how proud they are of the pupils' achievements in planning and problem solving despite their young age.

Citizenship is very much alive here, with a transparent democratic process in which pupils have a real say in decisions about their surroundings. The school places great value on their school council and makes this apparent. For example, school council

members were presented with their badges by the Mayor at the Town Hall. The pupils have also worked on real projects with the Botanic Gardens of Wales and are working as a partner with their town to achieve Fair Trade status.

community support

Penboyr Primary School have worked for nearly ten years to realise an ambitious dream of completely transforming their school grounds. It was, explained Headteacher Carol James, a project that was only realised through tremendous community support and which involved pupils in all aspects, from design to creation. Now pupils use their school grounds whenever they can and this has had a big impact on the curriculum. Displays around the school, for example, reveal how pupils have recreated the garden in sounds, written prayers and poems inspired by the garden, and produced pictures and plans depicting the varied characteristics of the site and new design ideas.

Local artists and poets have worked with pupils to create a sense of place. A beautiful and unusual tiled bench, with tiles hand-painted by the pupils, is the result of collaboration with a ceramics artist, and the distinctive school gates were made by a local blacksmith, following designs made by the pupils. This also involved a field trip to see the blacksmith making them.

Parents are enthusiastic, supportive and proud of what the school has achieved. Mothers Carol and Meirris had these comments to make:

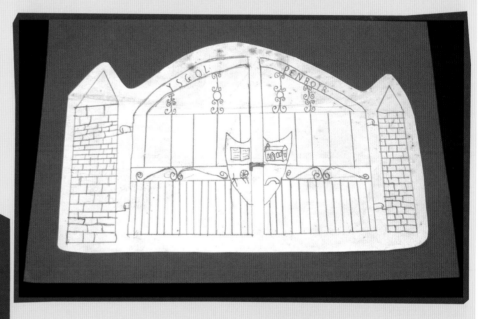

> It's a project that both parents and children have been able to join in with. A lot of parents were bringing all their children in and working as a family. Many members of the local community came along too as they had heard a lot about it.
>
> It's been good for getting to know other parents, working together and socialising. The school council approves lots of ideas so there's something going on all the time. We're already thinking about next year's planting, where to site a story-telling chair, and when to weave the willows. The children were so excited about the solar-powered water fountain!

Penboyr Primary School is also an Eco-School and has taken the principle of pupil and community participation to heart. The school's main achievement is in creating a much-valued curriculum resource through campus development with community support – an example of a balanced approach to practical ESD.

sustainable sense

Saron Primary School is in an former mining area of Wales. Its pupils have worked hard to improve their school grounds, gaining three Green Flag awards from the Eco-Schools scheme. Headteacher Gill Easton said that pupils and staff have made the best use of limited resources by planting and using reclaimed and recycled materials. The work at Saron has spanned at least ten years, producing many changes in the school grounds, and pupils have always played an important part in both planning and physically changing the landscape of the school grounds.

The construction of a nature trail was just one of the activities. It includes 18 different areas of study, such as a log pile, formal borders and a pond. A path meanders through a mix of woodland, marshland, a dry bank area and along the school field. Pupils have the opportunity to experience a miniature version of the countryside within the school boundary. This resource is also open to the local community.

Engaging pupils with their surroundings and teaching them to actively use all their senses is an integral part of the school's ethos and the outdoor provision and its

use during the school day reflects this. David Samuels, leader of many of the environmental projects, observed:

> **Because of my own experiences as a child, with the freedom to go anywhere and use all my senses, what I want is for pupils to enjoy the simplicity of nature and to know that they're custodians of the environment.**

In the nursery, pupils play outside using a range of resources designed to encourage and sustain curiosity, vocabulary, and

multi-sensory engagement with their surroundings. The range of stimuli includes:

- sticks and masking tape to build shelters
- plastic bottles recycled as containers for different smells, such as herbs or freshly-pared lemon rind
- tyres re-used as herb gardens and spider habitats
- a woven willow shelter
- bubble-wrap plastic packaging wrapped around horizontal poles for 'popping'
- planted containers
- a musical rack of kitchen implements
- a colourful sculpture on the school fence made from junk materials

The grounds are always full of pupils working in different ways:

- a nursery teacher works with a group of four-year-olds to match samples of herbs on a sticky strip with actual plants. She explains how essential this kind of work is to develop vocabulary and sensory appreciation of the world around them.
- other young pupils lean into the spider habitat, laughing and talking about what they might find.
- a boy is busy watering plants.

- another group of four year olds are working with their teacher to identify objects that have been hidden in the environment that 'don't belong' and there is lots of excitement as pupils search high and low.
- an outside table accommodates a group of five-year-olds who are collecting, sorting and measuring leaves whilst some six-year-olds are busy making and photographing sculptures they have made out of natural found objects.

The school grounds is just one focus of the school's work in ESD but the very high importance they place on the combination of campus and curriculum work impacts on the entire community as pupils take attitudes and new behaviours home with them.

sustainable energy

making choices

Eastchurch Primary School in Kent encourages pupils to share responsibility for energy monitoring and use in and around the school. Pupils work together, and with parents and the wider community, to try to use energy wisely, and this is also built into the curriculum. In this example, the pupils begin to think about their role as decision makers.

Key ESD concepts
- citizenship and stewardship
- needs and rights of future generations
- sustainable change
- uncertainty and precaution

Subject links
- geography
- science
- literacy
- citizenship

Other links
ECM 3: Enjoy and achieve
ECM 4: Make a positive contribution
ECM 5: Achieve economic well-being
Personalised Learning: Pupils develop responsibility for their own learning through being empowered to deliberate and decide actions which affect their future.

Planned outcomes
- Citizenship and stewardship: understanding the power of choice that we have in many aspects of everyday decision making; opportunities to actively practice decision-making skills.
- Needs and rights of future generations: knowing that our energy comes from using natural resources.
- Sustainable change: growing awareness of how reducing our energy consumption in school can benefit ourselves, others and the environment; an appreciation that using less energy can also be financially rewarding.
- Uncertainty and precaution: understanding why we should use energy more wisely.

Other geography outcomes
- Developing confidence in asking geographical questions about our everyday lives and actions
- The careful use of films to gain information about energy issues in other countries
- Making links between our own energy use and global effects

Essential resources
- A selection of energy appliances
- Recent school bills for heating
- Data loggers would also be useful
- 'Making Choices': one of a number of free teaching resources from the Ashden Awards website, which also has downloadable lessons, notes and films for use with interactive whiteboards. Short films about sustainable energy issues also include a pupil-friendly introduction to global warming, some school solutions showing pupils at work and numerous examples of small community solutions around the world.

Starting points
Eastchurch Church of England Primary School has elected energy monitors in every class, supported by an elite 'E-Team' who record weekly school energy readings and report on good practice by individual classes. The class monitors' job is to remind everyone to reduce their energy use wherever possible, e.g. turning off lights when leaving the classroom, ensuring computers aren't left on standby and doors are kept closed in cold weather. All energy monitors collaborate with the school council, and their work is valued in school and celebrated in the wider community. As this type of thinking was so clear in the school ethos it was important to make it more explicit in the

formal curriculum and staff had been keen to build practice into planning.

Year 1 pupils had already investigated energy, watched the Ashden introductory film on climate change, and discussed different kinds of fuel and how their use might affect the environment. The teacher drew on these prior experiences to re-affirm why it was important to use energy wisely and to gauge pupils' current thinking. Many pupils knew that it was important to try to use less energy and some knew it could save you money and that it was good for the environment. The teacher wanted pupils to think about ways in which energy use could be reduced and why it was desirable to do this, but most importantly, she wanted them to recognise that they have the power to make certain choices and are participants in daily life, rather than travellers through it.

Prompt questions
- What is a choice?
- What things do we choose to do?
  - e.g. What do I eat?
    What do I spend my pocket money on?
    Who do I play with?
    What do I do when I get home from school?
- Who decides?
- What things in our classroom use energy?
- What kind of fuel do you think is used to make our electricity?
- What kind of fuel runs our school boiler?
- How much do you think it costs?
- Why should we use energy wisely?
- When is energy being wasted?
- What actions can we take to reduce energy use?

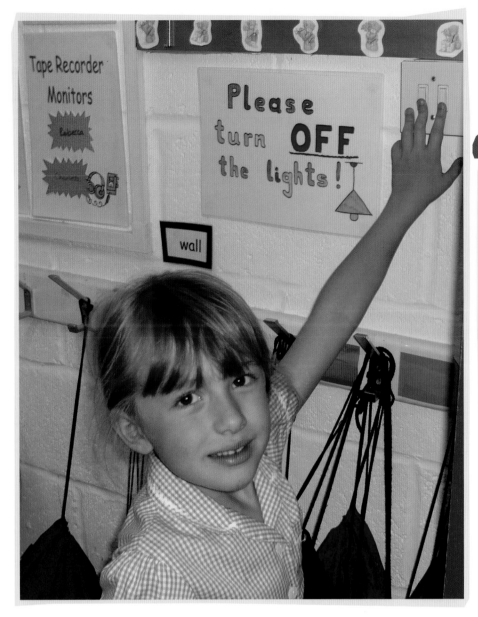

oil and gas to release energy in a very short period of time that puts too much carbon dioxide into the atmosphere and upsets the balance.

Talking about choices
Teacher Hannah Hobday explained:

> " We began by discussing what 'a choice' meant and making sure that everyone understood. The Ashden PowerPoint was adapted so that it had an image of one of our own pupils on the IWB to prompt ideas about choices we can make in our everyday lives. Initially some pupils said that their Mum or Dad told them what to do but after careful questioning, they realised that they could think of lots of examples of when they made choices for themselves. We then developed the discussion to focus on what we could choose to do regarding energy use in the classroom. "

Pupils were asked to identify the choices they make for themselves in everyday contexts, using a mix of probing questions, discussion time with peers, and class feedback to get this started and sustain responses. The pupils were quite surprised to realise that they 'chose' to do many things and some pupils could also give some simple reasons for making choices, e.g. 'because I like it', 'because it makes me laugh'. A few were even able to identify simple consequences of their choices, e.g. 'I choose to save my pocket money so I can buy a computer game'. Making the link between everyday actions and outcomes in such an explicit way helped pupils to start thinking about their potential to influence future events. This 'futures-orientated' thinking is an essential part of ESD and something that even the youngest pupils can do in supportive contexts.

Energy in the classroom
Although the pupils had already been taking steps to save energy in the classroom, such as switching off lights and shutting doors behind them, after watching one of the Ashden films about energy monitors in action, they were asked to discuss in groups how well they thought they really saved energy and how they could improve. Then the groups were given a chance to report back to the rest of the class before writing/drawing the choices that they would make regarding wise energy use.

Activities

Making a difference
The pupils had previously watched *Making a Difference*, a short film about climate change, and discussed some of the issues raised. This lesson was an opportunity to recap and check understanding as well as correct any misconceptions. Understanding how using energy from fossil fuels contributes to global warming is complex and cannot be covered in one lesson. Rather, it involves ongoing discussion and education.

Although there are still critics who believe that global warming is a concept that has been exaggerated, most eminent scientists, not least those who make up the Intergovernmental Panel on Climate Change (IPCC), agree that the current unprecedented and rapid rate of climate change is due to man-made causes, especially the burning of fossil fuels such as coal, oil and gas. So when pupils discuss the energy used for lighting, heating and powering appliances in their school and at home they should be able to make the connection between energy consumption, the fuel needed to produce it and, if fossil sourced, the effect on the planet.

So an essential starting point is to challenge the pupils to explain connections between types of fuel and energy use. This enables the teacher to re-establish with the pupils that most of the energy used by the school comes from power stations running on fossil fuels (coal, oil or gas) and that if we can use less of it then we will be helping to make our planet a better place to live.

When introducing the term 'carbon dioxide' to pupils it is important not to give the impression that it is a gas that is always damaging to life on Earth as, of course, it is a natural part of all life cycles. It should be explained to pupils that life on Earth is carefully balanced and that too much of anything in the wrong place can cause problems. It is the burning of lots of coal,

Hannah explained:

" Some pupils were challenged to use the internet and books to research an oral presentation which was filmed so that pupils could review themselves. Next year, we thought we might also give a presentation to parents or governors as the pupils enjoyed this activity.

We thought of questions about good energy housekeeping that we could ask other classes and our local council. This made the learning very relevant and purposeful and the pupils felt that their new knowledge was very important. "

All pupils were asked to keep an energy diary during half term with help from their parents. We sent a formal letter to parents and a simple diary format for pupils to use. This received a positive response from the local community, and some pupils carried out their own research on energy saving ideas. We are now going to share our ideas in a newsletter to parents. Projects such as this one are never really finished however, as there's always a new challenge just around the corner.

Challenges

Challenges for pupils

There were many challenges for pupils in this activity because they had to think about and make personal decisions, work collaboratively, consider how they could improve what they already did and how they could communicate effectively with others. It was a creative and critical process because pupils had to think about a range of ideas and then decide what they could practically do and how they might do it.

Challenges for teachers

"All pupils at our school are engaged in energy-reducing activities and are very vigilant, policing each other and staff with great enthusiasm. We have to 'walk the walk' as well as 'talk the talk'. I have had my laptop switched off by over zealous pupils when briefly leaving the classroom at lunchtime, even though I had planned to come back and work on it, so we have had to have discussions about considering other people's plans and being polite and courteous to avoid conflict. This has been a useful further direction for pupils and has extended their thinking while keeping myself and other teachers keenly aware that we are role models and co-collaborators.

I don't, however, want to be accused of indoctrination so I always remind pupils to ask others what they think and to respect their views because they will often see things differently. We have talked about what we could do at home to save energy but also about how we should talk to parents about it. This is another challenge – working with parents rather than against them – so we have tried to involve them in our discussions whenever possible. I want the pupils to know that we always have to be prepared to listen to others as we don't always know all the facts, and if we're not sure, we have to think about how we can find out what's right.

I also want pupils to make the connection between their everyday actions and life in distant environments so we plan to continue this learning through finding out about small communities around the world and their work on sustainable energy. This should enable pupils to have empathy with energy issues in other places and realise that their actions affect the whole planet."

Pupils' voices

This is one example of pupils' conversations, showing how much they were thinking and challenging each other:

I choose to turn the computer off

I'm going to make sure the door's closed when we go out to play

computers use lots of energy

Switch the door off!

Doors don't use energy.

The cold air gets in.

I don't understand ... about doors

Yes and energy gets out!

(There is a lull as pupils think about this and the teacher chooses to intervene)

"How do we keep our classroom warm in winter?"

We have a ... a radiator.

"And how do we heat up the radiator?"

Energy!

"That's right, from the school boiler. So what happens if we let cold air in from outside and let our lovely warmed-up air out?"

We get cold?

"Yes, the temperature drops in here ... so how do we get warmed up again?"

Put the radiator on more and have more energy?

"Yes that's right, we need more energy to make it warm again."

Where does the hot air go?

Teacher reflections

"Energy and climate change are very difficult concepts for young children to get to grips with. Nevertheless, our pupils had already had some input on both of these concepts, and although it will be a long and ongoing task for them to understand more fully, they are already engaged and that's the important thing.

We had already done some work on electricity so the pupils were confident in making connections between energy use and switching appliances off but as the conversation [left] demonstrates, some pupils found it harder to make other connections about energy use without some supportive scaffolding. Once the right questions were asked they made the connections easily.

The film we chose to watch was a good starting point as it engaged and excited pupils, and the visual stimulus helped them to grasp the complex ideas. It also helped me to provide for a variety of learning styles. I also made personalised materials for the pupils, for example, using photographs of people who are important and familiar to them in the school to help illustrate the concept of choice and what choices we can make to help save energy. I also used photographs of the pupils on the activity sheet that they completed at the end of the lesson and this attention to detail made them really excited and motivated them to try their hardest. Pupils who find it difficult to concentrate and who are not easily motivated showed high levels of both concentration and interest, and two pupils moved on to complete the harder task. The work produced was of a high standard and the pupils were very proud of it."

Futures thinking

All of the energy work carried out by the school is futures orientated because it has goals that are set in the future, i.e. to reduce energy use in practical and effective ways. This particular activity specifically links actions in the here and now with outcomes in the future through the concept of personal choice. It also makes the connection between local action and global outcomes and teaches pupils that our actions affect the environment at different scales of time and place.

Further ideas

Pupils at Eastchurch Primary School will be using their emerging skills to identify what makes a good energy monitor and individuals will decide if they want to stand for election, which requires giving reasons as to why they should be chosen. They will also be learning more about climate change and in particular how people around the world face energy challenges and devise sustainable solutions.

Assessment for Learning

Lessons that encourage discussion give opportunities for identifying what pupils know and what they think they know, and working with small groups enables supportive intervention to move thinking on. The collaborative nature of a common goal such as this also encourages a culture of critical peer support. These pupils had an opportunity to explain their 'choices' using their finished work which provided additional evidence of their thinking.

Why we chose this

Many schools have monitors with responsibility for energy, recycling or water but it is often an extra-curricular activity and not an active part of the school curriculum. Yet this kind of pupil participation is easily replicable, is a powerful motivator for learning and can fulfil many subject requirements.

References and further resources

www.ashdenawards.org/schools
The Ashden Awards support and reward sustainable energy initiatives. As well as the financial awards given to UK schools each year, there is also a wide range of free cross-curricular resources for primary teachers.

www.sustainablelearning.info/
Sustainable Learning is funded in England by the Department for Children, Schools and Families (DCSF), and in Northern Ireland by the Department for Education.

Schools in England will soon be rated on an A-G scale based on their energy efficiency, much like new fridges and washing machines. Sustainable Learning can help with this as the programme provides a structured, task-based approach to the way energy and water is used in schools. Schools already participating have reduced their energy use by an average of 10% and now have a better understanding of how energy and water is used in their schools.

www.create.org.uk
The CREATE Energy Links Library has a comprehensive and useful listing of energy, climate change related websites and resources.

Leading by example

Cassop Primary School has a long and successful history of making use of sustainable energy technologies and integrating them into the curriculum. The school has already replaced lightbulbs with energy efficient fluorescents before taking up an offer from Durham County Council to have a wind turbine installed in the grounds. The turbine generates about 50 MWh of electricity per year, which is more than enough to meet the needs of the school. As a lot of energy is generated out of school hours, some is also exported to the National Grid. In 2003, the old oil-powered boiler was replaced with an automated wood-pellet boiler, fuelled by locally produced wood pellets made from recycled waste wood. The school also boasts a photovoltaic (PV) array, mounted on a south-facing roof, which can gather energy from the sun and convert it into electrical energy even on cloudy days.

Headteacher Jim McManners explained:

> " The approach we take with our Early Years pupils is very much that of 'living what we believe in'. It is unlikely there would be a time when we would teach a lesson on being sustainable, but neither do we ever miss the chance in our conversations or through our actions to explain why we do what we do: why we have a turbine, why we grow our own food and heat the school with waste wood, etc. In parallel to this we try to provide every opportunity for pupils to be involved with their environment and for them to really enjoy and appreciate the natural world. We believe a prerequisite to saving the world is loving it! We want our pupils to be knowledgeable about their own environment, and by extension, interested and involved in the wider environment. This begins the moment they join us at the age of four and continues throughout their time at the school. "

As pupils progress through the school the technology is explained in more detail and it is continually emphasised why it is used. The pupils themselves become the ambassadors and the drivers of new initiatives. The concepts build throughout the school but are never taken for granted as there is so much misinformation available from all kinds of sources.

A small group of six- and seven-year-olds that came out with me today are now part of the way towards understanding why we have a turbine:

> " Why do you think we have our turbine? "

> TO make electricity

> So we don't run out of electricity

> " Also, when we make our electricity from the wind it doesn't put any nasty gasses into our air. Those gasses are making a mess of our air! "

> Yes, and so are those trees when they drop their leaves!

> "
>
> **Work in progress!!**
> "

caring for the future

Seaton Primary School in Devon has the motto 'Caring now for the future' which is well illustrated in the many active ways in which pupils work to make it a more sustainable institution. Seaton is one of the growing number of schools to have installed a range of renewable technologies; their 2.5kW wind turbine and 4.7kW PV array on the roof have enabled them to reduce their carbon dioxide emissions by around two tonnes per year. Like Eastchurch School, they have class 'Energy Agents' who lead the way in reducing energy waste. There is also an after school club which monitors overall energy use and produces a yearly energy audit which, by keeping everyone aware of energy use, has helped to considerably reduce overall energy consumption.

making big savings

Woodheys Primary School in Sale, Cheshire, has an excellent and efficient programme of practical energy saving methods throughout the school which it has successfully built into the school curriculum. The school has a solar PV array with an electronic display so that pupils can easily monitor energy generation, and energy efficient actions over past years have reduced gas consumption by 30%. The school also has 'Eco-Monitors' who encourage all pupils to be energy conscious, and believes it is very important to take messages of good practice back to homes and the local community. In this way, pupils have been encouraged to become good role models for their local community.

Travelling to School

Power to the pupils!

This wonderful example from Geddington Primary School shows how to involve pupils in a local problem that has both local (health and safety) and global (climate change) implications for sustainability.

Key ESD concepts

- interdependence
- citizenship and stewardship
- quality of life, equity and justice

Subject links

- geography
- literacy
- numeracy
- PSHE and citizenship

Other links

ECM 1: Be healthy
ECM 2: Stay safe
ECM 4: Make a positive contribution
SEAL: Pupils gain a real sense of agency in this example, learning that they have the power to make a difference to people's lives. This contributes to the motivation and social skills aspects of the SEAL programme.
Personlised Learning: Although the issue of congestion was initially a worry to the headteacher, the pupils quickly adopted it as their concern. Their personal stake in the outcome and direct connection to the topic meant that learning was real, meaningful and resulted in higher levels of achievement.

Planned outcomes

- Interdependence: understanding that what people do, including own activities, affects self, local environment and other people; being aware of the human changes in the local built and natural environment and beginning to understand some of the reasons for these changes.
- Citizenship and stewardship: knowing how to care for self and others, and for the home, school and local environment; ability to discuss things liked and disliked about the local environment and suggest ideas for looking after it.
- Quality of life, equity and justice: understanding the basic difference between needs and wants.

Other geography outcomes

- Know what the area outside the school is like
- Know how traffic affects the area outside the school
- Identify which times of day have the most traffic congestion
- Be able to explain why that is the case
- Be able to use and make maps and plans (to show where traffic is worst)
- Take responsible action to either walk to school or have parents park away from school gates whenever possible.

Essential resources

- School Travel Tool Kits (available to download from *www.saferoutestoschools.org.uk*).
- Large-scale maps and/or aerial photographs of the school and the road immediately outside the school. This helps pupils to locate where the congestion is and to record 'hot spots' such as where people park on the pavement.

Starting points

The pupils and staff at Geddington Primary School have always worked hard to care for the environment and decided to celebrate this by applying for an Eco-Schools Award. This national award is given to schools and their communities when they can show how they have improved their environment together. An obvious place for Geddington to start was to try to reduce the amount of traffic outside the school at the beginning and end of each school day.

Prompt questions

- How much traffic is there outside the school?
- How many cars, lorries, vans can you see?
- How can we keep count of the amount of traffic?
- How can we record traffic safely?
- Is there always the same amount of traffic?
- Are some times of the day busier than others?
- Which are the busiest times of day?
- Why are these the busiest?
- What happens when there is a lot of traffic?
- Where is the traffic worst?
- How many pupils in our school walk to school?
- Why don't more pupils walk to school?
- What can we do to help?
- What can our parents to do help?

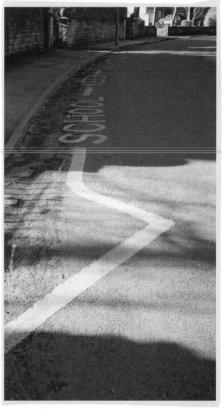

Activities

Key stage 1 pupils investigated how they travel to school, using the key enquiry question 'How does our journey to school affect our environment?'.

Getting to school

"We asked pupils to talk about their route to school, focusing on what features they see, e.g. junctions, main roads, pavements, traffic lights, roadworks, etc. We then looked at the different routes they take on a large-scale map of the area and discussed all the different forms of transport, when they might be used and by whom. This led to discussions about how the increase in traffic contributes to pollution and the use of energy. The class made a survey of the transport used to bring them to school."

Traffic congestion

The pupils observed that there was a lot of traffic around the school gates at certain times of day. They decided to do a survey of the amount/type/purpose of traffic outside school at different times and on different days. The results were displayed in graphs and charts.

"We talked about dangerous places/times and road safety. Photographs helped to prompt a discussion about different ways of improving congestion, such as traffic calming, zigzag lines, different layouts, pedestrian crossings, cycle routes and pedestrian routes. From this list of alternatives we discussed solutions for decreasing the traffic outside our school, such as walking to school, sharing transport, using public transport or cycling. These ideas supported the development of a school travel plan."

Asking others

A further idea might be to survey parents to see what other journeys they use their cars for (work, shopping, leisure). Can they consider any alternatives? (e.g. local shopping, shared use.)

Doing something about it

See 'pupils' voices' on p. 57.

Challenges

Challenges for pupils

There were two main challenges for pupils: first, the challenge of changing a habitual way of travelling to school. This was fine on the first few days when enthusiasm was high and the weather was fine but required more effort when the weather was poorer. Second, the pupils faced the challenge of how to encourage people to change their behaviour in a positive way. They realised that people are much more likely to respond to praise and rewards so decided that rewarding people for walking to school or parking further away from the school gates was a better course of action than punishing them for 'bad' behaviour.

Challenges for teachers

It is all too easy to provide pupils with answers to problems rather than allowing them to understand the problem and find solutions for themselves. Conducting the surveys was relatively straightforward, but generating alternative solutions and deciding which to select and how to go about it took a lot of skill. It was a balancing act: harnessing pupils' natural enthusiasm for their ideas and encouraging them to think through the effects of some of their suggestions (a good example of the need for both creative and critical thinking).

Since the establishment of the travel plan, the biggest challenge has been to ensure the changes are sustainable and not a 'one term wonder'. Involving parents and the local community was a crucial part of this.

Vocabulary

Traffic, transport, travel, routes, busy, quiet, parking, congestion, walking bus, pedestrian.

Pupils' voices

We decided to do something about the traffic outside our school as our headteacher had been very worried that a pupil would get hurt.

We watched from the hall window for 15 minutes, every morning, lunchtime and home time. We kept a survey for two weeks and then members of the Eco Committee drew a graph of the results. We could see straight away what the problem was: too many parents bringing their children to school by car!

We invited our community policeman into school to talk about road safety then we sent a newsletter to parents reminding them that the Highway Code states that they should not park:

- on a pavement
- nearer than 10m from a junction
- opposite zigzag lines.

We also sent them a map showing them all the places that they could park safely. We decided that parents are just like us and need to be rewarded for doing well so we thought hard about how we could do this and our campaign began...

At registration on certain days, we checked on how everyone had got to school. We gave out 'wonderful walker' badges to all those who had walked to school. As some people live outside the village and have to be driven to school, we also gave out 'perfect parker badges' if their parents had parked well away from the school gates. Everyone was really keen as badges build up towards prizes and we really noticed a difference in the amount of traffic. Many children told their parents where to park!

We also wrote to the local newspaper who wrote an article about us. Our local policeman said 'This is the best way I have ever seen traffic congestion dealt with, ever!'.

Teacher reflections

This extract shows just how motivated pupils were by this project. Devising positive ways of encouraging changes in behaviour and then seeing the results at first hand really amazed them and showed how it really is possible to make a difference. The levels of motivation in the classroom were high, and even pupils who normally struggle with more formal work were seen concentrating on their letters, badge designs and posters for sustained periods. It showed us just how powerful learning that involves curriculum, campus and community can be.

Futures perspectives

Thinking about the future was integral to this project as how pupils travel to school impacts on the future health and safety of both themselves and others in the community. This project also provides opportunities to extend thinking beyond the immediate local environment to the UK and out to a global scale, e.g. where are the areas with highest levels of car ownership and what might the impact of this be?

Further ideas

The next step at Geddington was to set up a walking bus:

> We sent a letter to parents about starting a walking bus. One of the mums who already walked to school with her children decided she would lead the bus. Pupils joined the bus at certain 'stops' along the route. Some of the older pupils and parents volunteered to become conductors. The safety tabards were not very popular, however, because the pupils thought they weren't 'cool'. With help, Mrs Holland designed some more trendy tabards, sashes and other reflective clothing which were much more popular. Mrs Holland has since won an award for her designs.

Inspection and Advisory Service as part of a series designed to address key areas of sustainable development in each year of the primary phase. Titles include: *Looking at Litter, Reducing Waste, Conserving Energy, Saving Water,* and *Thinking Globally, Acting Locally.*

Assessment for Learning

As teaching and learning about sustainable development does not often take place routinely across schools, a clear understanding of progression is crucial. Our assessment ladder (see p. 65) for the sustainable development strand of geography ensures that pupils are aware of what they are learning and what they need to do to make progress. This not only supports assessment for learning but is also a powerful planning tool for the non specialist.

Why we chose this

Traffic congestion is a common problem for almost all primary/infant schools. This is a wonderful example of how action can be taken to improve the situation without having to browbeat pupils or parents! Instead, the focus is on positive rewards not punitive action. This has led to a much more sustainable result as parents and the community as a whole have been motivated to take part.

References and further resources

Websites
www.eco-schools.org
www.safekidswalking.org.uk
www.walkingbus.com
How walking buses were established in St Albans, Hertfordshire.

Packs
Road Safety Education Toolbox (currently in all schools)

Fiction
Benet Richardson, J. (1992) *The Way Home.* London: Bodley Head Children's Books.
Burningham, J. (2002) *Mr Gumpy's Motor Car* (New Edition). London: Red Fox.
Gray, N. (2002) *A Balloon for Grandad* (New Edition). London: Orchard Books.
Nicoll, H. (2006) *Meg on the Moon.* London: Puffin.
Patten, B. (1995) *The Magic Bicycle.* London: Walker Books.

An extension from the walking bus is to incorporate learning from it into the classroom, e.g. physical health, pollution, reducing congestion, and, for older children, reducing CO2 emissions and climate change.

GRABB a bag (Geddington Rejects All Bad Bags)
Following a survey, pupils identified a need to reduce the number of plastic carrier bags being used. They secured a grant from the local council to buy re-useable cotton bags which were then printed with their own designs. Parents were expected to support the cause and even meet sales targets set by their children!

The medium term plans that inspired this example were devised by Alison Buckley, an Adviser with Northamptonshire

safety first!

South Avenue Infants in Sittingbourne, Kent, is located at a busy junction. Like most schools, they have a problem with parking at the start and end of the day. The year 1 pupils were embarking on a topic entitled 'How can we get to school safely?' and their teacher decided that pupils should have the chance to understand and tackle some of the problems themselves. An investigation took place in which pupils took part in several short field trips around the school perimeter where they:

- took photographs
- mapped the roads
- counted traffic at different times of the day
- learnt new vocabulary about road features and rules associated with road safety
- role played road safety in the classroom
- brainstormed what they had found out.

The pupils identified many problems and dangers, and thought of questions that would help them understand the situation better. These were put to parents and local residents who had been invited into school. Finally, pupils made recommendations, drew posters and sent advice home to parents, as well as giving a school assembly about the problems. They also decided to write a letter to the local newspaper to highlight their findings.

This is a good example of ESD as the learning was real and rooted in the everyday lives of the pupils. Despite their young age, they were able to identify that people were parking on double yellow lines, driving too fast and that there were too many cars on the road. This helped them to realise for themselves that it was better to walk to school if you could, and was a sobering reminder to some parents that their children knew where and when you could park safely. The work of these pupils also contributed to the school travel plan.

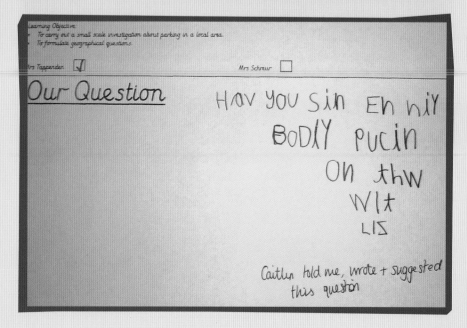

Learning Objective:
- To carry out a small scale investigation about parking in a local area.
- To formulate geographical questions.

Mrs Tapperden ☑   Mrs Schreur ☐

Our Question

Hav you sin Eh niy BODIY pucin On thw WIt LIS

Caitlin told me, wrote + suggested this question

Resources

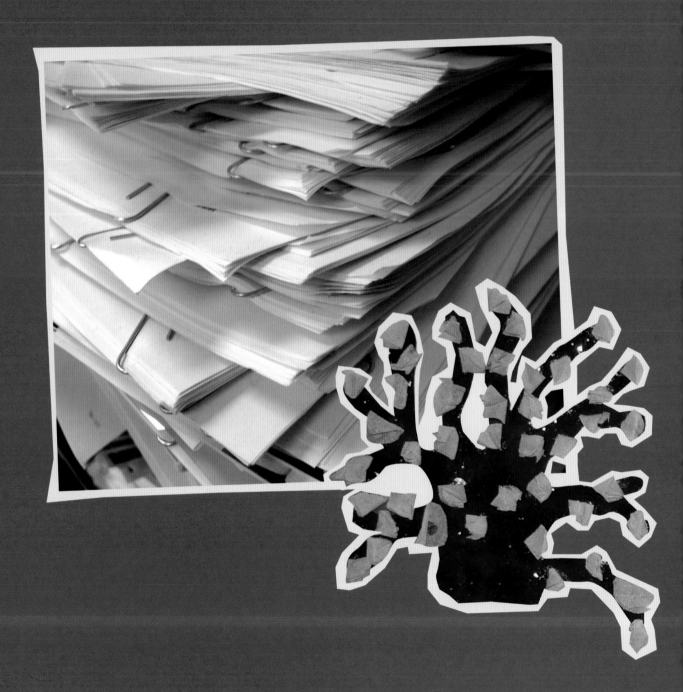

This section provides a short- and medium-term plan for ESD, a sustainability action plan, and an example of what progression might look like against the National Curriculum assessment levels. Each resource links to an example provided in the previous chapters.

Year: 2–6

Subject: Geography

Introduction: This is a one-day activity to promote the map making process at primary level. The activity can be undertaken in isolation of the existing geography work or can underpin a medium term plan based on graphicacy.

Learning objectives

- to understand the main features of a map
- to be able to make a journey stick of a route
- to understand that maps can show the route of a journey
- to make a map of a route taken with a journey stick

Cross-curricular objectives

- to respect the Countryside Code
- to be able to undergo peer assessment in a small group

Learning outcomes

Most pupils will know the main features of a map and will create a journey stick independently while observing the Countryside Code. They will recognise the features that the journey stick reminds them of and represent this on a map using most of the features discussed.

Lower ability: With support, pupils will create a journey stick and be able to transfer this into a linear map. They will create a basic map but this may be mainly pictorial and may not represent the full route taken.

Higher ability: Pupils will have an understanding of map making and will be able to give examples of both the features of a map and experiences when they have used a map. They will create a journey stick and a map that will reflect the journey accurately, with emoticons (emotion symbols) used to extend the map. They will support peers in assessing their maps and be able to recognise the skills they have acquired during the activity.

Resources

An open space; a class set of sticks; sticky tape; drawing pins; paper; wax crayons for tree rubbings; stickers to make emoticons; string.

Key vocabulary

- Map making (rather than 'map drawing' which suggests a more artistic and less geographical response to the task)
- Route
- Journey stick
- Linear map
- Features of a map, e.g. key, scale,
- Affective mapping

Session outline

Preparations

- In the classroom, begin with a discussion about 'what is a map?'. Ask pupils to identify the key features of a map (such as symbols, colour and scale) and to give examples of when they have used these features as part of map reading in their own lives.
- Ask pupils to consider how well they could make a map of a known area, such as the school and grounds, if you asked them to do so right now.
- Introduce the concept of a journey stick and explain the activities pupils will be undertaking.
- Look at the Countryside Code rules (available from *www.countrysideaccess.gov.uk/things_ to_know/countryside_code/educational _resources/educational_resources*) and discuss how pupils can work responsibly while making their journey sticks. You should also discuss the health and safety implications when picking things up, e.g. items they should avoid.

The journey stick

- Each pupil starts with an empty stick. As they walk around the area selected, they collect items that interest them, attaching these in chronological order to their stick with sticky tape, thus marking the journey they have taken. The items will be different for each pupil which

- Encourage pupils to talk to a partner about their linear maps. This begins the process of being aware that geography can be a personalised subject.

Map making

- Bring the class together and explain to pupils that now they have had a first attempt at making a map, they are going to twist and turn their linear map and journey stick to create a map of the area. (Although the journey stick will show the map as a straight line, the actual journey will have taken twists and turns so this map will be a more accurate locational map).
- Remind pupils of the discussion about features of a map and create a checklist for them to follow.
- All pupils then make a final map including a key and other features discussed. NB It is at this point that differentiation and scaffolding learning can occur.
- Extension: Encourage pupils to make their maps affective through the use of emoticons, which can be added to the key. Alternatively, they can create a living graph (Higgins and Baumfield, 2001) of their experience to discuss in the plenary.

Plenary

- Bring the class together and assess the maps through peer discussion.
- Ask pupils to work in pairs, and using the checklist created prior to the map-making, ask them to assess each other's maps.
- Bring the class back together and discuss:
  - Did anyone see a map that had included all the points on the checklist?
  - Why was each map different?
  - How did the journey stick help you to make a map?
  - What have you learnt about the skills you can practice in geography from doing the journey stick activity?

Reference
Higgins, S. with Baumfield, V. (2001) *Thinking through Primary Teaching*. London: Chris Kington Publishing.

With thanks to Dick Palfrey of Kirklees Education Service who ran a workshop on journey sticks at the 2005 Charney Manor Conference.

For more ideas see www.teachers.tv/video/23949 where a 15-minute film shows geography specialist Jane Whittle as she leads her class on a magical journey through their school grounds.

should encourage a sense of personal geographical experience.
- As the pupils attach their items they begin to realise that the stick is representing the whole journey and that the order in which they attach their items signifies this. For example, if there is a half way point on the walk, pupils know that this should be marked with an object at the central point on their stick.
- In order to make the journey sticks affective, emoticon stickers can be used.

Linear map
- Following completion of the journey stick, pupils can remain in the area or return to the classroom.
- Ask them how long they think professional mapmakers take to produce a map and if they think it is drawn in one go. Explain what a linear map is, and that they are going to make one to show what they found on the route.
- While drafting the linear map pupils can add emoticons.

Medium-term Plan: Appledore Community Primary School and Nursery curriculum planning

Term: Autumn 2007
Year: 1
Overall theme:
The world around me
1. Growing up (8 days)
Visit: The Life Skills Bus

'Thinking Actively in a Social Context' (TASC) wheel
Oxfam 'A curriculum for global citizenship'

The key elements for responsible Global Citizenship

Knowledge and understanding
- Social justice and equity
- Diversity
- Globalisation and interdependence
- Sustainable development
- Peace and conflict

Skills
- Critical thinking
- Ability to argue effectively
- Ability to challenge injustice and inequalities
- Respect for people and things
- Co-operation and conflict resolution

Values and attitudes
- Sense of identity and self-esteem
- Empathy
- Commitments to social justic and equity
- Value and respect for diversity
- Concern for the environment and commitment to sustainable development
- Belief that people can make a difference

This material is taken from *Education for Global Citizenship: A Guide for Schools* (2006), with permission of Oxfam GB, Oxfam House, John Smith Drive, Cowley, Oxford OX4 2JY, UK www.oxfam.org.uk/education. Oxfam GB does not necessarily endorse any text or activities that accompany the material.

Outcomes covered

Every Child Matters	Stay safe	Enjoy and achieve	Positive contribution	Economic well-being
SEAL		New beginnings	Say no to bullying	Getting on and falling out

Knowledge and understanding of the world
(Geo, Sci, MFL, DT, RE, His)

The Life Skills Bus
My wonderful body: explore how the body works; balanced diets; medicine safety; and personal hygiene.
(Sci 2, 1b, 2a, 2b, 2c)

Ourselves
Identify and locate parts of the human body, including sense organs.
(Sci 2, 1b, 2a, 2b, 2c, 2g, KO)

Brain Academy
Plan an investigation to see if the tallest pupils in the class are also the oldest.
(Sci 1)

Where in the world is Barnaby Bear?
Where did pupils go for their summer holidays? Locate countries on world map and make own passports (to include key features, e.g. height, colour of hair, eyes, etc.)
(Geo 3a, 3b)

Naming parts of the body in another language
Learn the names for key body parts in chosen MFL and then play games using these.
(MFL 3g)

Creative development
(Art, Mus)

Singing
Sing songs about the parts of the body, e.g. 'Heads, Shoulders, Knees and Toes' or 'B-O-N-E-S' (Sung to tune of 'B-I-N-G-O'):

'Once there was a skeleton,
And Bones was his name, oh!
B-O-N-E-S, B-O-N-E-S, B-O-N-E-S,
And Bones was his name, oh!

Once there was a skeleton,
And Bones was his name, oh!'
B-O-N-E-(clap),
B-O-N-E-(clap),
B-O-N-E-(clap),
And Bones was his name, oh!'

(Repeat the verse but each time drop one more letter and add a clap until the entire name is clapped.)
(Mus 1a)

Portraits
Explore ideas about self-portraits. Investigate and use drawing and painting materials and techniques to communicate ideas.
(Art 1a, 2a, 2b, 3a, 4a, 5a)

Physical development
(PE)

Leap into life
Gymnastics, games, athletics
(PE)

Dance
Links with science work on the five senses.
(PE 6a, 6b, 6c)

Swimming
Weekly session at local pool.
(PE 9a, 9b, 9c, 9d)

Range of activities in the jungle area:
blindfold trail, hoop circle, human alphabet, arrow trail, the really wild hunt trail.
(PE 11a)

Personal, social and emotional development
(PSHE, citizenship)

Child protection
Keeping oneself safe (links with drugs education)
(PSHE 3a, 3f; Sci 2d)

Safety education
Keeping safe indoors and outdoors (links with class and school rules).
(PSHE 1e, 2d, 3g)

New beginnings
Belonging: Pupils learn that they belong to a community; they feel safe and content within the class. (SEAL 1f)

Choices
Pupils discuss their likes and dislikes, and the difference between right and wrong.
(Citizenship 2c)

Communication, language and literacy
(Eng, ICT)

Class rules (week 1)
To make a booklet on the agreed class rules.
(Eng 3, 1b, 1d)

Otherwise (film clip) (week 2)
Think about how others in a group are feeling, especially when one person looks very different.
(Eng 1, 1a, 2a, 3a, 4a)

Labelling the parts of the body
Move key words to correct part of the human body (using textease).
(ICT 3a)

- **Role play**
The health centre
(Eng 1, 3e, 4a)

Reasoning, problem-solving and numeracy
(Ma)

Measure
Use standard and non-standard units to measure height, weight, etc. of individuals.
(Ma 3, 4a, 4c, KO)

Data handling
Put class data into a bar graph and make observations of the results.
(Ma 2, 5a, 5b)

Record data results in tables
(Sci 2, KO)

KO: Knowledge and Understanding of the World